A TEACHER'S GUIDE TO

writing
CONFERENCES

— Grades K–8 —

Carl Anderson

series editor **KATIE WOOD RAY**

Heinemann • Portsmouth, NH

Heinemann
361 Hanover Street
Portsmouth, NH 03801–3912
www.heinemann.com

Offices and agents throughout the world

Photograph on page 68: © Hero Images / Getty Images

Library of Congress Cataloging-in-Publication Data
Names: Anderson, Carl, author.
Title: A teacher's guide to writing conferences / Carl Anderson.
Description: Portsmouth, NH : Heinemann, [2018] | Series: The classroom essentials series | Includes bibliographical references.
Identifiers: LCCN 2018015480 | ISBN 9780325099187
Subjects: LCSH: English language—Composition and exercises—Study and teaching (Elementary) | Creative writing (Elementary education) | English language—Composition and exercises—Study and teaching (Middle school) | Creative writing (Middle school) | Teacher-student relationships.
Classification: LCC LB1576 .A535 2018 | DDC 372.6/044—dc23
LC record available at https://lccn.loc.gov/2018015480

Editor: Katie Wood Ray
Production: Hilary Goff
Cover and interior designs: Vita Lane
Typesetter: Vita Lane
Illustrator: Anzia Anderson
Photography and videography: Sherry Day, Michael Grover, Dennis Doyle, David Stirling
Manufacturing: Steve Bernier

Printed in the United States of America on acid-free paper

22 21 20 19   VP   2 3 4 5

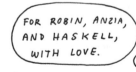

FOR ROBIN, ANZIA, AND HASKELL, WITH LOVE.

book
MAP

1
What Is a Writing Conference? 1

Start by Discovering What the Student Is Doing as a Writer . . . 22

About the Videos in This Book

By viewing the video in the online resources, you can watch me confer with writers in a range of grades who are writing in a variety of genres. Along with each conference, you'll find a video commentary from me that will help you better understand the teaching you see.

Across the chapters in this book, whenever you see this icon , I've identified specific conferences that will help you envision the work you are reading about at that point. Some conferences are referenced multiple times for different reasons, and whenever I can, I give you a grade range of conferences to choose from to illustrate the same idea.

While I don't have conferences to represent every possible aspect of conferring, you'll see a wide range of common situations that will help you imagine conferring with your own students. Sometimes, you'll watch an entire conference clip, so you can see how a concept plays out across the writing conference. Other times, you might choose to watch just part of a clip as you study one of the three parts of a writing conference. Or you might simply use the descriptions to choose conferences that interest you before or after you dig into the reading.

VIDEOS

To access the online videos, visit **http://hein.pub/ClassroomEssentials-login**. Enter your email address and password (or click "Create New Account" to set up an account). Once you have logged in, enter keycode **CECONWRIT** and click "Register."

GRADE	STUDENT	DESCRIPTION OF CONFERENCE
K	Massimo	Massimo is writing a nonfiction book. I teach him how to develop details by labeling his illustrations.
1	Ariana	Ariana is writing a nonfiction book. I teach her to elaborate by adding "action facts."
1	Jovani	Jovani is writing a nonfiction book. I help him learn how to write a new lead by studying a mentor text.
1	Liam	Liam is writing a nonfiction book. I teach him to capitalize the first letter of each sentence.
1	Urijah	Urijah is writing a nonfiction book. I teach him to elaborate by including "number facts."
2	Jackson	Jackson is writing a personal narrative. I teach him how to write precise character actions.
2	Shelby	Shelby is writing a nonfiction book. I teach her to elaborate by adding "action facts."
2	Skyler	Skyler is revising a personal narrative. I teach her to use "revision tools" to add on to her draft.
3	Addison	Addison is writing a review. I teach her to analyze the mini-stories she has included to develop her reasons.

GRADE	STUDENT	DESCRIPTION OF CONFERENCE
3	Billy	Billy is writing about an opinion. I teach him to elaborate on his reasons by writing about hypothetical situations.
3	Sage	Sage is writing about an opinion. I teach him to elaborate by writing precise examples.
4	Lucine	Lucine is writing a personal narrative. I teach her to punctuate complex sentences.
4	Matthew	Matthew is writing about an opinion. I teach him to elaborate by including examples.
4	Sam	Sam is writing about an opinion. I teach him how to write a counterargument.
5	Kiely	Kiely is writing a memoir. I teach her to write a reflective ending.
5	Ginger	Ginger is writing a memoir. I teach her to develop important scenes.
5	Shreya	Shreya is writing a memoir. I teach her to write a reflective ending.
6	Aden	Aden is writing a personal narrative. I teach him how to edit for spelling mistakes.
6	Elsa	Elsa is writing a memoir. I teach her to develop scenes by writing character actions.

GRADE	STUDENT	DESCRIPTION OF CONFERENCE
6	Emily	Emily is writing fiction. I teach her to cut an unnecessary part.
6	Logan	Logan is writing a book review. I teach him that writers can begin a review by introducing their perspective on the book.
7	Connor	Connor is writing fiction. I teach him how to make a plan for his story.
7	Grace	Grace is writing fiction. I teach her to include telling character details.
7	Henry	Henry is writing a literary essay about *The Odyssey*. I teach him how to develop his analysis of the text.
7	Maggie	Maggie is revising her fiction story. I teach her how to make a revision plan.
8	Ari	Ari is writing a fantasy story. I teach him to develop the interior life of his characters.
8	Sofia	Sofia is writing fiction. I teach her to develop her theme by including specific events about her characters' lives.
8	Theo	Theo is writing a memoir. I teach him to include details that develop his main point.

1

WHAT IS A writing CONFERENCE?

My First Writing Conference Was a Disaster

No one has a gene that makes him or her good at conferring. Most of us, in fact—even the most skilled among us today—have failed in our first attempts at conferring with our young writers.

In the fall of 1987, I was a second-year teacher at an elementary school in the Bronx. I had read about writing workshop in Lucy Calkins' book *The Art of Teaching Writing* (1986), and I was especially intrigued by the writing conferences she described in its pages, which seemed like an excellent way to teach my students, who had such diverse needs as writers.

After I gave my first minilesson and my students began writing, I looked around my classroom until my eyes settled upon Syeda, a thoughtful, studious girl. I imagined that if I sat down and conferred with her, she would probably say something smart and interesting about what she was doing as a writer—just like the children in the conferences that Calkins had described in *The Art of Teaching Writing*—and that in response I would have the opportunity to teach her something important.

I walked over to Syeda's desk, knelt down next to her, and smiled. She stopped writing and looked up at me nervously. I asked, "How's it going?"

Syeda said nothing. Instead, she looked at me as if she were a deer caught in headlights. Unfazed, I glanced at her writing and asked, "How's it going with *your writing*?"

Syeda looked at her writing for a moment, then back at me. Finally, she answered my question. "Mr. Anderson, it's going . . . okay," she said.

I felt disappointed—and panicked. Syeda hadn't shared anything about what she was trying to do as a writer and thus hadn't given me any direction about what I might teach her in the conference. Since I didn't know what to do next, I ended the conversation by saying, "Syeda, I'm really glad it's going okay." Then I walked back to my desk and sat down, wondering about what had gone wrong and unsure of what I could do to have better conferences.

Like all of us who start conferring with student writers, I had a lot to learn to be more successful. I needed to understand the underlying principles that shape writing conferences, as well as the teaching moves that experienced writing teachers make in conference after conference. That's what this book is for—to introduce you to the principles and moves of good conferring. So, if you're ready, let's get started.

Writing Conferences Happen in Writing Workshop

You'll confer with your students in writing workshop. To demystify the term *workshop*, think about its definition: a place where people are doing some kind of work. (In Santa's mythological workshop, for example, elves are making toys!) A writing workshop, then, is a place where students are doing the work of composing pieces of writing and, through daily practice and instruction from their teacher, becoming better writers.

Each day in writing workshop, you'll confer with students as they work on pieces of writing connected to the current unit of study, in whatever stage of composing they're in. Your units of study will focus on genres of writing (Allyn 2012a, 2012b; Calkins and colleagues, 2013, 2014; Robb 2012) or other aspects of writing such as how to "read like writers" (Ray 1999), how writers use punctuation (Angelillo 2002; Feigelson 2008), or how to be independent writers (Cruz 2004).

During a unit of study, students in primary grades usually fill up their folders with numerous pieces that may take one or a few days each to complete. Students in upper elementary or middle school write a few pieces—or sometimes even just one piece—in a unit of study, since the pieces they write are longer and more complex and take more time to complete.

Q&A

HOW MANY CONFERENCES SHOULD I HAVE EACH DAY?

ANSWER: Plan for four to seven minutes per conference, and then about one minute per student for taking notes and also for a quick check-in with each student later during the period. At that pace, you should be able to have four conferences a day if students have thirty minutes of independent writing time. If you decide to meet with a small group, you'll have fewer conferences that day.

A writing workshop consists of these three parts:

1 *Minilesson (10–15 minutes):* A whole-class lesson about a writing strategy, craft technique, or language convention. In many classrooms, the teacher has students gather in the meeting area for the minilesson.

2 *Independent writing (25–30 minutes):* Students work on their writing back at their seats. The teacher walks around the classroom and has several writing conferences with students, which usually last 4–7 minutes each.

3 *Share session (5–10 minutes):* The class reconvenes to discuss how writing went that day, either to highlight (student) work or to give feedback to a few students about their draft-in-process.

What Is a Writing Conference?

A Writing Conference Is a Conversation . . .

A writing conference is, first and foremost, a conversation. The word *conversation* suggests so many things about the way you should talk with students.

Invite students to have a real give-and-take with you.

Even though in conferences you're a teacher talking to students, you're also a (more experienced) writer talking to (less experienced) fellow writers about what writers do—come up with topics, make a plan for a piece of writing, write a lead, develop a section with detail, use commas in a series, and so on. In this give and take, you learn about what students are trying to do as writers and how well they're doing it, and the students learn how they can do their work better.

Speak in a conversational tone.

Tone is the foundation of the good relationships you want to develop with students over the course of the school year. Speaking in a warm, friendly manner puts students at ease and makes it more likely they will talk with you about what they're trying to do as writers. What you learn from this talk helps you assess students and decide what you should teach to help them grow.

Sit alongside students, at their eye level.

How you sit with students helps you establish a positive tone in conferences. You might grab a nearby empty seat or sit on one that you carry with you around the classroom. As you sit, it's important to make frequent eye contact with students and make sure that your facial expressions show an interest in what students are telling you.

Use "active listening" strategies.

For example, give some wait time after asking a question so that students have the time and space they need to come up with a response. Ask students to "say more" about what they tell you. And repeat what children say to check that you're hearing them correctly. Using these strategies shows that you have a real interest in what students are saying and that you're really trying to understand them. Students will usually respond by talking to you more.

VIDEOS

Massimo, Grade K

Shelby, Grade 2

Matthew, Grade 4

Sofia, Grade 8

WORDS FROM
A TEACHING MENTOR

[Conferences] are not mini-lectures but the working talk of fellow writers sharing their experience with the writing process.

—DON MURRAY, 1985

If we can keep only one thing in mind it is that we are teaching the writer and not the writing . . . If the piece of writing gets better but the writer has learned nothing that will help him or her another day on another piece then the conference was a waste of everyone's time.

—LUCY CALKINS, 1994

. . . That Teaches Students to Be Better Writers

The goal of a writing conference is to teach students something about writing that they can use in the future. If you add to students' writing repertoires in every conference, they become better writers over time.

It's important that you teach students about **one** aspect of writing in each conference. This one aspect could be

- *a strategy for navigating a stage of the writing process,* such as how to come up with a topic or edit a draft

- *a craft technique,* such as how to write an effective beginning (or lead) for a piece of writing or use transitions

- *a point of grammar or mechanics,* such as how to punctuate a sentence with a period or set off a dependent clause with a comma.

If you try to teach two or three things in conferences, they will go on for too long—and students won't be able to take in so much teaching, no matter how well-intentioned. Helping students grow as writers is a long-range project. Across a school year, you'll have many writing conferences with students—and whatever you don't address in one conference can always be a focus later.

VIDEOS

Skyler, Grade 2

Connor, Grade 7

Urijah, Grade 1

Logan, Grade 6

Liam, Grade 1

Lucine, Grade 4

TIP

Interruptions break the "flow" of conferences and prioritize one student's needs over another. To minimize interruptions:

- Explain the importance of conferences to your class and point out that you shouldn't be interrupted except under the most serious circumstances, such as if a student is feeling sick.

- Signal students not to interrupt. For example, you might give a quick shake of your head if you see students approaching during a conference, or you might wear a "conferring hat" that signals that you shouldn't be interrupted.

Teaching students to be better writers requires that you learn to navigate the three parts of a writing conference. Within each part, there are one or more conferring moves you'll learn to make by using intentional language.

PARTS OF A CONFERENCE

CONFERRING MOVES

INTENTIONAL LANGUAGE

DISCOVER what the student is doing as a writer.

ASSESS how well the student is doing what he's doing, then DECIDE what to teach him.

TEACH the student how to do what he's doing better.

Invite the student to tell you what he's doing as a writer.

- Listen to what the student says about what he's doing.
- Look at the student's writing.
- Decide what to teach.

- Give feedback.
- Teach.
- Coach.
- Link to independent work.

"How's it going?"

"Let's take a look at your writing . . . "

- "I want to give you some feedback . . . "
- "I'm going to teach you . . . "
- "Let's try that together . . . "
- "Now I want you to try what we talked about on your own . . . "

3 Ways Conferences Get Sidetracked

1. Sometimes teachers get mesmerized by what students are writing *about*. They end up having long conversations with one student about her vacation to Myrtle Beach and another student about his opinion that NCAA athletes should be paid for playing on their college sports teams. As fun and interesting as these conversations can be, they do little to help children grow as writers.

2. Other times teachers have trouble resisting the urge to jump in and fix something in a student's draft that's bugging them. For example, they find it hard to bite their tongues when they can come up with the perfect ending for a student's piece, and so they tell the student how they think it should go. However, when teachers take control of a student's writing like this, all they've done is given a demonstration of their expertise. We shouldn't confuse this with helping students develop their own expertise.

3. Finally, when some teachers see that students have many issues as writers, they feel driven to point all of them out, much like their own teachers once took red pens and corrected all the errors in their writing. The problem with responding to student writing like an editor is that in reality, editors work with people who already know how to write. When an editor makes suggestions to a writer, she can safely assume the writer will know how to make the improvements. But students are apprentice writers, and we can't expect that naming issues in a draft is the same as showing students how to address them.

> ## WORDS FROM A TEACHING MENTOR
>
> **When a teacher confers with a writer, her interactions tend to follow a consistent pattern, one that teachers of writing have deliberately chosen and that reflects many beliefs about learning, teaching, and writing development.**
>
> **—LUCY CALKINS, 2013**

> **The teacher cannot always simply focus upon the students' work—either product or process— and expect growth and success. More often than not, interpersonal relationships have a profound effect on the student's motivation and work.**
>
> —DOUGLAS KAUFMAN, 2000

Why Confer?

We Confer to Develop Relationships with Students

Most teachers understand intuitively that the quality of the relationships they have with students has a big impact on their learning. In classrooms filled with many children, it's challenging for teachers to develop relationships with students. Fortunately, in a writing workshop, writing conferences give you this important opportunity.

When you ask the question, "How's it going?" at the beginning of writing conferences, you're doing much more than inviting students to talk about what they're doing as writers. The question initiates your relationship with each student and deepens each of these relationships in subsequent conferences.

In conferences, the student becomes *known* to you as a person, a writer, and a learner. As you come to know each child, you shape and adjust your teaching for that child.

Students, too, learn a lot about you in conferences. Through conferring, you become *known* to your students. For most students, getting to know you helps them be more comfortable and open to learning in conferences.

The relationships that grow out of writing conferences are not the by-product of conferring—they are one of the important goals, since these relationships are so central to students' growth as writers.

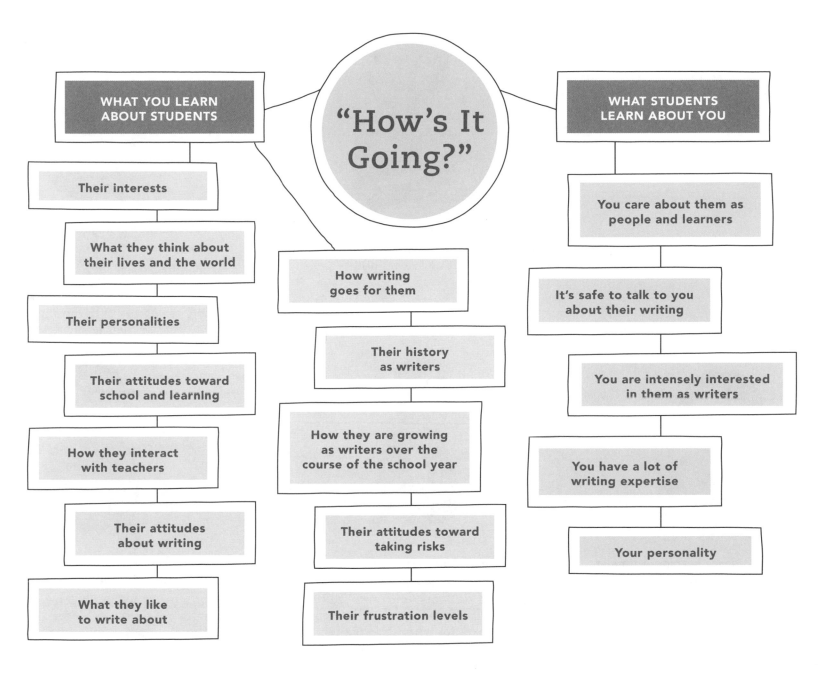

"How's It Going?"

WHAT YOU LEARN ABOUT STUDENTS

- Their interests
- What they think about their lives and the world
- Their personalities
- Their attitudes toward school and learning
- How they interact with teachers
- Their attitudes about writing
- What they like to write about

- How writing goes for them
- Their history as writers
- How they are growing as writers over the course of the school year
- Their attitudes toward taking risks
- Their frustration levels

WHAT STUDENTS LEARN ABOUT YOU

- You care about them as people and learners
- It's safe to talk to you about their writing
- You are intensely interested in them as writers
- You have a lot of writing expertise
- Your personality

We Confer Because Each Student Is a Different Kind of Writer

When you look around at the students in your classroom, it can be daunting to consider how many ways they can differ from each other as writers and learners. But when you confer, you learn lots of things about your students that will help you support their individual needs:

The student's attitude toward writing.

While some students enjoy writing, others don't.

The student's motivation for writing.

Some students often have a real purpose for writing—for example, to try to right a wrong in society or to make their classmates chuckle—while others write simply to comply with the expectations of their teacher.

The student's tendency to enjoy writing in some genres, but not others.

Some students prefer writing fiction but don't care much for writing literary essays.

The student's writing experience.

In a fifth-grade class, there may be some students who have been in writing workshops since kindergarten and others for whom this is their first writing workshop experience.

The student's strengths in some aspects of writing and weaknesses in others.

One student will write long, detailed drafts but have trouble focusing her material; another will write a focused draft that's short on detail.

The student's knowledge of craft.

Some students, either as a result of instruction or from "reading like a writer," have a deeper knowledge than other students about the craft of writing.

The student's knowledge of the language system.

Some students know a lot about grammar, punctuation, and spelling and are able to produce drafts with few errors, while others write drafts that have many errors.

The student's fluency in written English.

Many classrooms today contain a mixture of children for whom English is a second language and children who are native English speakers.

The student's special needs.

Some students have physical, developmental, behavioral, or sensory special needs or a combination of several of them.

The student's attitude toward taking risks.

Some students will try new things eagerly, while others are more reluctant, sometimes because they are afraid to fail.

The student's frustration level.

Some students get frustrated easily when trying something new that's challenging; others rarely do.

We Confer to Help Students Make Good Choices

Since Don Graves first wrote *Writing: Teachers and Children at Work* (1983), one of the bedrock principles of writing instruction has been student *choice*. Experienced writers make numerous choices every time they compose a piece, so to become good writers, students need experience making these same choices.

Let's think for a moment about some of the more important of these choices. Students need experience choosing

- their own topics for writing

- the purpose for their writing and the genre that best fulfills that purpose

- what meaning to get across about the topic they have chosen

- strategies to navigate each step of the writing process

- when to move from one stage of the writing process to the next

- the ways in which they craft their writing

- the audience for their writing and how to write their drafts with that audience in mind.

> **WORDS FROM A TEACHING MENTOR**
>
> Every child [has] behavioral characteristics in the writing process that applie[s] to that child alone.
>
> —DONALD GRAVES, 1981

But just because students are given the opportunity to make choices doesn't mean they will always make good ones. To learn to make good decisions, students need a lot of guidance from you as they're in the process of making choices about their writing.

When you confer, there are three ways you can help students learn to make good choices:			
IF YOU LEARN . . .	**FOR EXAMPLE . . .**	**THEN YOU . . .**	**BY . . .**
The student has made a good choice.	She is writing a dialogue lead to her story, which is a powerful way to begin.	Teach her how to follow through on the choice she has made.	Showing her the craft moves in a dialogue lead in a mentor text.
The student could have made a better choice.	The student has a topic for his argument, but he's picked it because he thinks it will please his teacher.	Teach him how to make a better choice.	Sharing a strategy for finding personally meaningful topics.
The student hasn't made choices an experienced writer would have made at that stage of the writing process.	The student says she's finished, even though she hasn't made any revisions to her draft.	Teach her to make some new choices.	Demonstrating a revision strategy, such as how to add details to her piece.

Q&A

AT WHAT POINT (OR POINTS) IN THE WRITING PROCESS SHOULD I CONFER WITH STUDENTS?

ANSWER: Students need to get better at all aspects of writing if they're going to grow as writers; thus, you should have conferences at *every* stage of the writing process.

Because some teachers are uncomfortable when students publish flawed pieces, they confer only *after* students have finished revising and editing, to help them "fix up" their writing. Remember, however, that the goal of conferring is to help students become better writers. If you teach a first grader how to write with specific detail, you've helped her become a better writer. But many first graders spend just a few days on a piece of writing, so you probably won't confer with her again about that piece. And it's bound to have several flaws—after all, the student is six years old! You have to make peace with this inevitability. Even if you teach eighth graders, who may spend several weeks composing a piece of writing, you will be fortunate to have two or three conferences with them during that time. Their final pieces, too, will have flaws.

Feedback was among the most powerful influences on achievement. Most programs and methods that worked best were based on heavy dollops of feedback.

—JOHN HATTIE, 2009

We Confer to Receive and Give Feedback

Feedback is a key to student learning. Since writing conferences are conversations between students and teachers, they provide opportunities for two types of feedback: student to teacher, and teacher to student.

The powerful thing about the feedback loop is that assessment and teaching happen in *real time*. In conferences, you listen to students talk about their writing, you look at students' work, and then you teach in response to what you've learned. As the school year progresses, feedback is also informed by what you have learned *across time* about students and how they're growing and changing as writers. And, as soon as a conference is over, students can act on the feedback they've received from you *immediately*.

Where the student is in the writing process, and what she thinks she needs to do in that stage or the next

What is going well for the student

What is going well for the student as a writer

Any problem(s) the student is having

What the next step is for the student as a writer

What minilessons the student is trying

What writing goals the student is working on

How the student is crafting her draft

What strategies the student is using

TEACHER TO STUDENT FEEDBACK

STUDENT TO TEACHER FEEDBACK

TIP

What you learn about students' needs in writing conferences also helps you make decisions about which students to place in small-group lessons. Small groups are most effective when students have similar needs.

We Confer to Inform Whole-Class and Small-Group Instruction

Today, you have access to an abundance of curricular materials. You can easily acquire excellent units of study for narrative, informational, and persuasive genres. While these units are wonderful starting places if you're new to the teaching of writing or to teaching a particular unit, they do present a dilemma: although the authors of these units are very knowledgeable, they cannot predict with certainty the mix of learners in classrooms where their units will be used. Hence these authors cannot predict with confidence every lesson that should be included in units, how many days to spend on them, or even their order.

By conferring with several students a day in writing workshop, you're able to see what learning "trends" are occurring, and revise your unit plan accordingly. In some cases, a trend may become obvious as you move from conference to conference during a single workshop. Other times, you'll notice a trend when you reread your conferring notes after several days' worth of conferences.

WORDS FROM A TEACHING MENTOR

As you teach the unit, you will make decisions that will alter the path of your teaching. You may decide to add a minilesson topic or take one out. You might decide to spend more or less time on a topic. You might decide to teach a lesson earlier or later than you had anticipated.

—MATT GLOVER AND MARY ALICE BERRY, 2012

Whenever you notice a trend, you can revise a unit of study accordingly:

WHEN YOU NOTICE THIS TREND . . .	YOU CAN REVISE YOUR UNIT BY . . .
Students are having more difficulty than expected with a recent minilesson.	→	Giving another minilesson (or more) on the same topic.
Students are excited about a recent minilesson.	→	Devoting more minilessons to exploring the same topic.
Students are able to do something that's the focus of an upcoming minilesson.	→	Cutting the minilesson from the unit.
Students are interested in an aspect of writing that's not in the unit plan—for example, a craft they noticed in a mentor text.	→	Adding a minilesson (or more) to the unit about this aspect of writing.
Some of the lessons that were placed later in the unit seem more relevant to current student needs.	→	Changing the order of the minilessons in the unit.

Q&A

WHERE SHOULD I CONFER WITH STUDENTS?

ANSWER: Go to where your students are sitting—their tables or desks—or have them come to a special conference table. Each location has its advantages.

CONFERRING WHERE STUDENTS SIT

ADVANTAGE 1
Students will be more at ease on "their own turf."

ADVANTAGE 2
Students' materials—their writing folders, writer's notebooks, pencils, pens, folders, alphabet charts, and so on—are on their desks and easy to access during a conference.

ADVANTAGE 3
It's easy to invite nearby students to listen in on the conferences.

ADVANTAGE 4
As you move from one student to the next, you can redirect students you notice need refocusing.

CONFERRING AT A CONFERENCE TABLE

ADVANTAGE 1
If you have physical limitations, conferring in one spot may be easier for you.

ADVANTAGE 2
All of your necessary conferring "tools"—note-taking forms, mentor texts, and so on—are laid out on the table, ready to use as needed.

ADVANTAGE 3
When the conferring table is placed right in the middle of students' desks or tables, the teacher's presence helps with management.

TIP

Use these strategies to help students work independently so you can confer:

- Spell out (in minilessons) exactly what students are expected to do during independent writing time.

- Point out writing supplies and tools and describe how students are to access them.

- Establish procedures so students can go to the bathroom without having to get permission from you.

- Teach strategies for how to get started with writing each day.

- (In primary) Teach students strategies for spelling unfamiliar words and composing sentences.

- Explain what to do when a piece is finished.

- Use revision and editing checklists to help students revise and edit on their own.

- Teach students to have peer conferences, look at mentor texts, or read charts that summarize recent minilessons when they need help.

- Ask students to make plans for independent writing time. Primary students can "turn and talk" to a writing partner and discuss their plans at the end of the minilesson. Upper-grade students can do the same or jot down their plans in their writer's notebooks.

- Designate the first five minutes of independent writing time as "no walking, no talking" time to give students a chance to settle in to their writing without distraction. You might play some calming music during this time.

- In between conferences, do a quick walk around the room so you can redirect any students who have become distracted.

- If your class is getting noisy, ask students to stop writing so you can report on what you just taught in a conference, and suggest that some students try it themselves. This is a positive way of refocusing your class!

See Leah Mermelstein's *Self-Directed Writers* (2013) for more ideas about how to keep students working on their own.

START BY DISCOVERING
WHAT THE
student
IS DOING AS A
WRITER...

In the first part of a writing conference, find out which stage of the writing process the student is in—rehearsal (or prewriting), drafting, revising, editing, or publishing. Also, determine what kind of writing work the child is doing at that stage.

PARTS OF A CONFERENCE

DISCOVER what the student is doing as a writer.

ASSESS how well the student is doing what he's doing, then DECIDE what to teach him.

TEACH the student how to do what he's doing better.

CONFERRING MOVES

Invite the student to tell you what he's doing as a writer.

- Listen to what the student says about what he's doing.
- Look at the student's writing.
- Decide what to teach.

- Give feedback.
- Teach.
- Coach.
- Link to independent work.

INTENTIONAL LANGUAGE

"How's it going?"

"Let's take a look at your writing . . ."

- "I want to give you some feedback . . ."
- "I'm going to teach you . . ."
- "Let's try that together . . ."
- "Now I want you to try what we talked about on your own . . ."

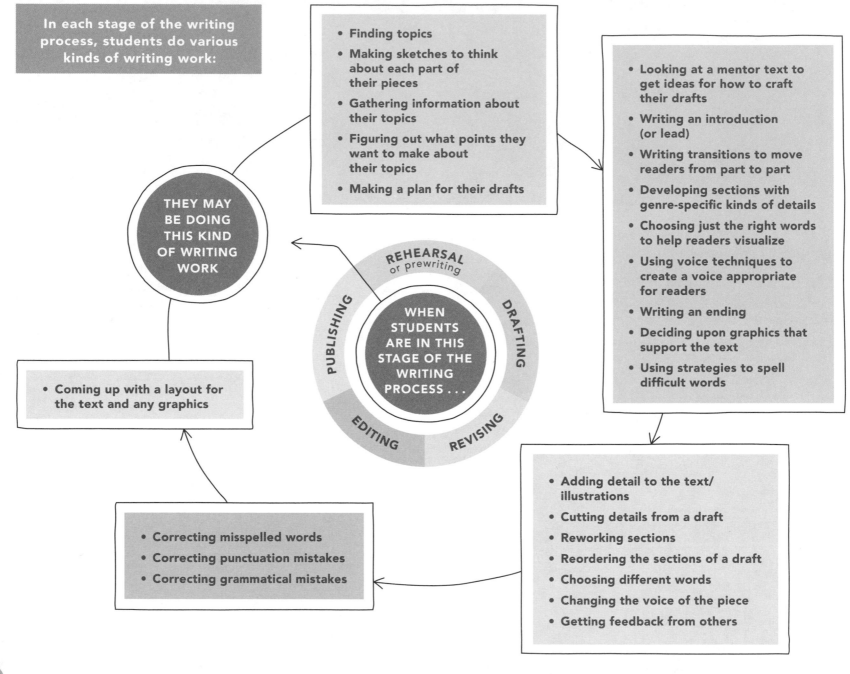

In each stage of the writing process, students do various kinds of writing work:

THEY MAY BE DOING THIS KIND OF WRITING WORK

- Finding topics
- Making sketches to think about each part of their pieces
- Gathering information about their topics
- Figuring out what points they want to make about their topics
- Making a plan for their drafts

WHEN STUDENTS ARE IN THIS STAGE OF THE WRITING PROCESS . . .

REHEARSAL or prewriting

DRAFTING

REVISING

EDITING

PUBLISHING

- Looking at a mentor text to get ideas for how to craft their drafts
- Writing an introduction (or lead)
- Writing transitions to move readers from part to part
- Developing sections with genre-specific kinds of details
- Choosing just the right words to help readers visualize
- Using voice techniques to create a voice appropriate for readers
- Writing an ending
- Deciding upon graphics that support the text
- Using strategies to spell difficult words

- Coming up with a layout for the text and any graphics

- Correcting misspelled words
- Correcting punctuation mistakes
- Correcting grammatical mistakes

- Adding detail to the text/illustrations
- Cutting details from a draft
- Reworking sections
- Reordering the sections of a draft
- Choosing different words
- Changing the voice of the piece
- Getting feedback from others

Invite Students to Talk About Their Writing

Begin conferences by asking students an open-ended question that invites them to talk about what they're doing as writers. Don Murray (1985) made the question, "How's it going?" a favorite way for teachers all over the world to begin their writing conferences. You can also start conferences with one of these questions:

- What are you doing as a writer today?
- What's up with your writing today?
- Could you tell me about the writing work that you're doing?

Students learn quickly that these questions are cues for them to talk in one or more ways about what they're doing as writers. For example, in the beginning of this conference, the student, a fifth grader, talks about the revisions she is making to her historical fiction story:

GRADE 5

TIP

I recommend you start conferring almost immediately after the minilesson. If your first conference is with a student who's just getting started, chances are she has writing from the previous day(s) that can be the focus of your conference. Or ask her what she plans on doing that period, and then teach in response to those plans.

TIP

When you confer with students who are new to writing conferences, they may respond to the opening question by telling you about what happens in their story or about interesting facts in their all-about book or feature article. When this happens, try gently interrupting them ("Okay, thanks for telling me some of the story about your dog"), reflect back what you've heard them say ("I can tell that your dog does some funny tricks!"), and then redirect them to talk about what they're doing as writers ("So what are you doing as a writer today?"). Of course, if students are writing about something emotionally difficult for them, react with empathy ("I'm so sorry your dog died.").

After you ask the opening question, it's important that you are quiet and look at students with a sense of expectation that they will respond. Don Graves (1983) recommends that teachers wait as long as ten to fifteen seconds after they open a conference for students to respond. While this may seem like an eternity, the silence gives students time to think about what to say. And it communicates a message that they have a responsibility to hold up their end of the conversation and that you have faith that they can do so.

When students talk about what they're doing as writers, they

- give us insight into what they are trying to do. What a child says helps us answer the question, "What do I teach this student today?"

- set the direction of the conference and take responsibility for their own learning. Conferences give students agency as writers and learners.

- think about what they are doing as writers and, more importantly, why. They become more deliberate writers and become more aware of what they're doing, both in the moment and over time.

- learn to ask the question, "How's it going?" themselves and use it to self-monitor how they're doing with a piece of writing.

- develop a life skill that will benefit them as students, workers, and citizens. In *The Global Achievement Gap*, Tony Wagner (2008) names "oral (and written) communication" as one of the "Seven Survival Skills" that students need to develop to be successful in the twenty-first century.

TIP

To use the precious time you have for conferring, make a plan for who you will confer with each day so that

- you won't waste time after each conference trying to decide who to see next

- you'll be better able to say no to the student who wants to have a conference with you every day

- you won't overlook the quiet students.

Scan your class roster and select students for that day's conferences. Usually, you'll choose students you haven't seen in a while. Occasionally, you'll select students because you know they have difficulty navigating a particular point in the writing process. For example, students who have trouble with organization often benefit from conferences when they are starting drafts.

CONFERENCE RECORD

Student	Dates										
Syeda	9/8	9/25	10/2								
Edward	9/13	9/27	10/3								
Stacey	9/11	9/18									
Raymond	9/14	9/19	10/4								
Haskell	9/12	9/20									
Damya	9/14	9/28	10/5								
Anzia	9/12	9/27									
Nate	9/11	9/25									
Tiffany A.	9/14	9/18	9/28	10/2							
Jemel	9/8	9/29									
Demeka	9/13	9/20	10/4								
Ethan	9/14	9/25	10/5								
Leo	9/11	9/27	10/3								
Kamara	9/15	9/18									
Micah	9/13	9/29									
Tiffany N.	9/15	9/27									
Wyatt	9/8	9/19	10/2	10/5							
Josh	9/15	9/29									
Aurora	9/11	9/20	10/4								
Kaelyn	9/8	9/26									
Henry	9/15	9/25									
Bonnie	9/12	9/18	9/20	10/5							
Malika	9/12	9/29	10/2								
Sylvie	9/13	9/26	10/4								

What Will Students Talk About?

When you begin a conference with "How's it going?" you hope that students will respond with the kinds of talk that writers engage in when they talk about their work. If you keep these kinds of talk in mind as you confer, you'll know what to listen for as a child speaks. Of course, the sophistication of this "writing talk" will depend upon the student's age and writing experience. Students might respond in a number of ways, as shown in the next several pages.

Students Might Name the Genre They're Writing

This kind of talk is often the very first kind that we hear from primary writers. Students are becoming aware that there are different kinds of writing, and they are beginning to envision different ways that writing can go.

In order to have a clear vision for their writing, it's important that students have a strong sense of genre and can name what they're writing with precision (instead of calling everything a "story"). Knowing what genre students are writing is also helpful to you, since it narrows down the things you might teach.

Students Might Describe Where They Are in the Writing Process

GRADE 3

Students might name the stage of the writing process they are in and/or the kind(s) of work they're doing in that stage. Or they'll talk about how they're about to move into the next stage. Sometimes they'll summarize the work they've done in several stages.

GRADE 5

Students Might Discuss What They Think Is Going Well in Their Writing

GRADE 1

GRADE 7

Students Might Name a Problem They're Having with Their Writing

Q&A

WHAT ABOUT STUDENTS WHO REQUEST CONFERENCES?

ANSWER: Students who request conferences are learning how to advocate for themselves and their needs, which is an important aspect of becoming an independent writer. You could post a conference sign-up sheet, check it each day to see if any students have signed up, and then decide to revise your conferring plan to accommodate them. Make sure it's clear that you can't always confer with students who sign up.

On the other hand, some students will stop working and request conferences as soon as they run into trouble. In primary classrooms, students who want their teacher's help will sometimes form a line behind her as she moves around the room, a phenomenon I call the "Make Way for Ducklings syndrome." Discuss with your students what they can do when they experience difficulty—ask a classmate for a peer conference, look at mentor texts, use writing tools like the word wall or dictionaries—and tell them they should reach out to you only after they've tried problem-solving on their own.

Students Might Describe How They're Solving a Problem

GRADE 2

GRADE 6

Students Might Explain How They're Crafting Their Writing

GRADE 2

Craft talk—that is, how students are using techniques such as strong leads and endings, kinds of detail, and word choice—will come up in many conferences. You'll hear this kind of writing talk when students are drafting and revising.

GRADE 4

Students Might Discuss the Meaning They're Trying to Get Across in Their Drafts

GRADE 2

Since writing is fundamentally a meaning-making and meaning-communicating activity, it's exciting when students share what they're trying to say about a topic in their texts, or tell you that they're trying to figure this out.

GRADE 8

Students Might Talk About How They're Using Conventions

GRADE 1

While younger students might bring conventions up at any point in the writing process, older students who have learned that writers edit toward the end of the writing process are most likely to talk about conventions while they are editing.

GRADE 6

Students Might Name the Goals They're Trying to Achieve

This kind of talk tends to happen in classrooms where teachers set goals for students and/or teach students how to have their own writing goals, what those goals can be, and how to work on them over time.

Students Might Talk About Their History and Growth as Writers

WORDS FROM
A TEACHING MENTOR

When teachers seek . . . feedback from students as to what students know, what they understand, where they make errors, when they have misconceptions, when they are not engaged— then teaching and learning can be synchronized and powerful. Feedback to teachers helps make learning visible.

—JOHN HATTIE, 2009

Q&A

WHY NOT FOCUS ON THAT DAY'S MINILESSON IN EVERY CONFERENCE?

ANSWER: Minilessons are planned to address the needs of many students and propel them forward in the work of the study. Conferring, on the other hand, is differentiated instruction. You may find that a student is already able to do the work of the minilesson, or that he's not yet ready for it, or that there is something else that makes more sense to teach him at this moment in time.

Five Scenarios That Happen After You Ask, "How's It Going?"

Students respond to the question, "How's it going?" in different ways, and how you proceed with a conference depends on the response. Luckily, the different kinds of student responses are fairly predictable, and once you learn to recognize them, you can be more strategic about how you engage students.

Scenario One: The Student Tells You Something He's Doing That You Want to Get Behind

Ideally, students quickly identify and explain what they're doing as writers, and you decide to get behind it and support it.

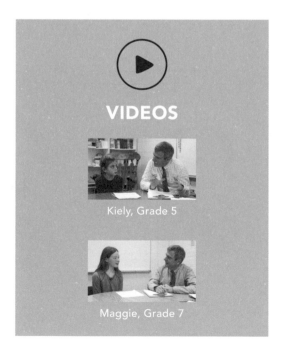

VIDEOS

Kiely, Grade 5

Maggie, Grade 7

There are several good reasons to get behind what a child is doing. Sometimes, more than one of them will apply in a conference.

1. **The student has a problem that must be solved before he can move forward.** For example, he's having trouble picking a topic or spelling challenging words.

2. **The student is trying out a recent minilesson.** If the focus of the minilesson is something that you know a student needs or something that can take her in an important new direction, you might get behind the work.

3. **The student is doing something you know he needs to get better at.** What the student is doing matches a goal you've set for him that's based on your previous assessment, such as writing with precise detail or using end marks consistently.

4. **The student is trying to do something that you want students in his grade to learn to do.** Grade-level expectations are spelled out in district and state standards, as well as in some published writing curriculums, such as Lucy Calkins and colleagues' *Units of Study in Opinion, Information, and Narrative Writing* (2013) and *Units of Study in Argument, Information, and Narrative Writing* (2014), which contain grade-level "progressions." Because some students will be writing either above or below grade level, you need to have the expectations for higher and lower grades in mind as you confer.

5. **The student is showing a lot of energy for what she's doing.** Sometimes a student has her own agenda and is super-enthusiastic about something she's doing—something to encourage in all writers.

Although students will sometimes tell you enough for you to decide to get behind what they're doing, you may need them to be more specific to help you know exactly where to go with the conference. For example, a student tells you he's "adding details," but you need him to talk more precisely to decide what aspect of detail to teach him.

Use these three strategies to help students talk with more precision about what they're doing: ask students to *say more*, ask follow-up questions, and name what students are doing.

VIDEOS

Skyler, Grade 2

Elsa, Grade 6

Sofia, Grade 8

Strategy One: Ask Students to *Say More*

Questions such as "Could you say more about that?" and "What do you mean by that?" nudge students to keep talking and often get them to reach for more specific language that will help you know exactly what they're doing.

Strategy Two: Ask Follow-Up Questions

Asking students questions about what they're doing is another way to get them to say more and give you more specific information. Based on what the student has told you, use your knowledge about the kinds of specific work writers do in different stages of the writing process to ask logical follow-up questions.

The teacher knows that there are different kinds of details writers use as they craft their texts, so she follows up with a question that asks the student to be more specific.

VIDEO

Maggie, Grade 7

TIP

You can also use these three strategies in Scenarios 2 and 3 to help students talk with precision once you've helped them name something they're doing that you want to get behind.

Here are examples of follow-up questions you might ask students when they're in different stages of the writing process. Remember that the lines between the stages are permeable and the student may be moving between them.

KEY

Stage of the Writing Process

What the Student Might Say

Questions You Might Ask in Response

I've picked a topic.

Why did you choose this topic?

Are you writing about a writing territory or favorite topic?

I don't know what to write about.

What strategies do you usually use to find topics?

I'm writing about my topic in my writer's notebook.

What strategies are you using to write about the topic?

What point do you want to make about this topic?

I'm getting ready to start my draft.

What strategies are you using to get ready to write? Talking it out with a friend? Sketching across the pages of your book (primary)?

What kind of plan have you made for your piece (upper)?

What's the focus of your piece?

How does each part of your plan help you get your focus across?

DRAFTING

I'm starting my draft.

How do you get started with a draft?

Do you have a mentor text that is helping you imagine how to write this piece?

I'm adding details.

What kinds of details are you using in this piece? Why?

Does one kind of detail seem especially important in this piece?

How are you writing exact, precise details?

I'm at the end of my draft.

What kind of ending are you writing? Why?

I'm stuck and don't know what to write anymore.

What do you do when you get stuck?

I'm using my plan to write my piece.

How have you organized your piece? Why?

What kind of lead are you writing? Why?

I'm working on word choice.

Why did you choose this/these words in this sentence/section?

REVISING

I'm revising.

What kinds of revisions do you feel your piece needs? Why?

How do you figure out what revisions you need?

Where have you revised already? Why did you make these revisions?

What mentor texts are helping you imagine the revisions you need to make?

What revision tools (sticky notes, footnotes, arrows, etc.) are you using?

EDITING

I'm editing.

What editing strategies are you using?

What kinds of mistakes are you finding? How are you correcting them?

I'm stretching out the important parts of my piece.

What are the most important parts of your piece? Why? What will you do to write them well?

I'm trying to get voice in my writing.

What voice techniques are you using? Why?

Where do you think it's most important to use voice techniques in your writing?

I'm using transition words.

What kinds of transitions are you using? Why?

Strategy Three: Name What Students Are Doing

Sometimes students don't have the writing vocabulary to "say more" with precision. When this happens—often with inexperienced writers and emergent bilinguals—and you think you know what the student is trying to say, you can name what she's doing and then check with her to see if you're right.

When the teacher restated what the student said, using the word *scene* instead of *part* and *dialogue* instead of *talking*, she used the vocabulary that experienced writers use, which the student will need to talk more precisely in the future. Thus, in conferences you also have an opportunity to teach students how to talk like writers.

Scenario Two: The Student Tells You Something She's Doing That You *Don't* Want to Get Behind

Sometimes when you ask "How's it going?" students will say the very first thing that comes to mind, even if there are other, more important things they're actually doing. Or sometimes they're not that experienced in talking about writing, so they tell you something they know writers do at some point in the writing process, but it's not necessarily what they're doing right now.

For a variety of reasons, you'll sometimes decide *not* to get behind what a student says she's doing because you believe it

- would be better addressed in another stage of the writing process. For example, she wants to work on fixing punctuation errors when she's at the very beginning of writing a draft.

- reveals that she's skipped a stage in the writing process. For example, she may tell you she's editing her writing but she hasn't made any revisions.

- isn't something she really needs right now as a writer, based on what you've learned about her so far. For example, she says she's working on her lead, but you know her most important need is organization.

- is something that she's actually doing well, and you don't see the need to teach her more about it. For example, she says she wants help with her counterargument, yet she's actually written a good counterargument that uses each craft move you pointed out in a mentor text during a minilesson.

VIDEO

Shreya, Grade 5

In these conferences, it's important to resist the impulse to get behind what students say initially. Instead, you might ask, "What else are you doing as a writer?" Often, this simple question will nudge students to think a bit more and then tell you something else they're doing, hopefully something you'll want to get behind. You could also use one or more of the strategies described in Scenario 3 to help students name something else they're doing, or read their writing, as described in Scenario 4.

GRADE 2

A Teacher's Guide to Writing Conferences

Scenario Three: The Student Initially Doesn't Say Much About What He's Doing

Let's be honest—not all kids respond helpfully when we ask the question, "How's it going?" They respond by saying that things are going "good" or "okay," or they shrug and say nothing at all.

There are many reasons why students don't say much:

- Some students are new to writing workshop—primary students, or older students who have never been asked to talk about the work they're doing as writers. Consequently, they don't yet have the writing vocabulary they need to talk about their writing work.

- Students who are English language learners can find basic conversational English to be a challenge, so the specialized academic language required to confer with a teacher can be even more challenging. In her book on writing workshop and emergent bilinguals, *From Ideas to Words*, Tasha Laman (2013) has some excellent ideas about conferring with emergent bilinguals. Danling Fu's *Writing Between Languages* (2009) is another good resource.

- Sometimes there are kids who are shy or who just don't feel like talking with you when you drop by for a conference.

- And sometimes middle school students don't really want to talk with adults, particularly in front of their peers.

Regardless of why students don't say much, you still need to find a direction for the conference. Here are six strategies to jump-start conversations and nudge students to say something you want to get behind.

Q&A

WHAT IF A STUDENT DOESN'T WANT A CONFERENCE?

ANSWER: Students will occasionally ask if they can postpone a conference to another time. They may be in a "writing groove" and not want to be interrupted, or they might be writing about something deeply personal. In these special cases, I recommend that you agree to meet with them on another day. However, while there will be times when students aren't enthusiastic about having a writing conference—they may be feeling badly about the writing they're doing, they may not be getting along with you that well at the time—I suggest that you not be deterred by their ambivalent reaction when you sit down next to them.

Strategy One: Ask Students to Look at Their Writing

Some students are able to start talking about their work after they've held their writing in their hands and looked it over for a few moments. The act of picking it up and flipping through its pages gives them some time to think and reminds them of the work they've been doing, or are thinking of doing.

GRADE 4

Strategy Two: Support Students with Specific Questions

Try asking a few of these specific questions that nudge students to talk in the ways that writers talk about what they're doing:

- In what genre are you writing? What are you doing to make this kind of writing?

- Where are you in the writing process? What are you doing at this stage of the writing process?

- What is your next step?

- What is going well for you as a writer today?

- Are you doing anything as a writer that feels a little bit hard today that I can help you with?

- What problems are you having, and how are you solving them?

- What recent minilessons are you trying out in your writing today?
- Are you trying anything you've seen in one of our class mentor texts?

- What do you want to say in your draft? What are you doing as a writer to get across what you're trying to say?
- Are you working on any of your writing goals today?

VIDEOS

Massimo, Grade K

Jackson, Grade 2

Ari, Grade 8

Strategy Three: Name What You Have Observed

Another way to get students to talk about what they're doing is to describe something you've observed the student doing.

GRADE 8

Strategy Four: Suggest Possibilities

Sometimes it helps to suggest things a student *might* be doing. Suggestions can come from

- what you know writers often do in a particular stage of the writing process
- recent minilessons you've given that the student might be trying
- things you've discussed with the student in previous conferences (refer to your notes).

VIDEO

Elsa, Grade 6

Strategy Five: Refer to a Chart of Recent Minilessons

In many classrooms, teachers make charts of the things students are learning to do during the current unit of study and then carry around mini versions of these charts when they confer. The language on these charts can help students find the words and phrases they need to talk about what they're doing in their writing.

WE ARE LEARNING THAT WHEN WRITERS WRITE STORIES, THEY . . .

- Focus on one (or just a few) parts of an event
- Write interesting leads

- Write character actions
- Write character feelings and thoughts

- Write dialogue
- Write setting details

- Write character descriptions
- "Stretch out" the most important part(s)

- Use time transitions
- Write interesting endings

GRADE 3

This strategy gives support to students who are new to speaking "writer's talk"—primary students, students new to writing workshop, emergent bilinguals.

Strategy Six: Take a Tour of the Student's Writing

Another strategy you can use to jump-start a conference is to "take a tour" of a student's writing—that is, quickly skim her writer's notebook or draft and look for evidence of the kinds of work she's doing. Has the student written just a few lines of her draft, indicating she's writing a lead? Are there arrows leading from the text to the margins, telling you the student may be adding information? Has the student circled misspelled words, indicating she may be editing for spelling? Once you think you know what work the student is doing, ask her to confirm your hunch.

GRADE 5

The "take a tour" strategy is particularly useful when you confer with primary writers, as well as emergent bilinguals in any grade. Especially at the beginning of the school year, when they haven't been immersed (yet) in much writing language in minilessons and conferences, the "taking a tour" strategy exposes students to "writing talk" they'll eventually start using themselves in conferences.

Jovani, Grade 1

Sam, Grade 4

Scenario Four: Ultimately, the Student Doesn't Talk About Something You Want to Get Behind—or Doesn't Talk About What He's Doing at All

In this scenario, you read the student's writing to figure out what he's doing. This can have some pitfalls, mainly that you might be tempted to focus on the first issue you see—which might not be the most important or appropriate issue to address. Also, since some students have so many issues as writers, you can feel overwhelmed when you look at their writing.

For these reasons, it's important to read students' work with these lenses:

- Do I see that the student is trying out something we discussed in a recent minilesson or, if she hasn't, that she could try it in this piece?

- Do I see that the student is trying out—or could try out—something that's connected to one of his needs as a writer?

Q&A

WHAT IF THE STUDENT HAS SO MANY NEEDS, YOU AREN'T SURE WHERE TO START?

ANSWER: Look for something to teach that's appropriate for the stage of the writing process the student is in. For example, if the student is drafting or revising, teach him one thing about focus, structure, or detail. If the student is editing, teach him how to correct one error that he makes several times in his piece.

Let's try this out by thinking about a conference with a fourth grader. Her teacher had been teaching the class to develop all the important parts of their drafts because she noticed this was something many of the students, including this one, needed to learn to do. Here's how the beginning of the conference went:

Now, sit in this teacher's seat and read the student's writing. As you read, look to see if the student develops all the important parts of her story.

The Poodle

"Are we there yet?"

"No."

"Are we there yet?"

"No."

"Are we there yet?"

"Don't even think about it, dear. We're almost there," my dad said in a tired voice.

We (my mom, dad, and two brothers) were on our way to my Grandmother's house and I knew I would get over my fear of dogs. We finally pulled into her driveway and I heard the dog barking. Maybe it's too early to get over my fear, I thought.

My Grandmother opened the door. I ran outside the car right up to the porch and into her house. I felt ashamed. My Grandmother and I were talking, but all I could think about was Boo-Boo the dog. The big, hairy, scary . . . labradoodle.

I know it's pathetic. I went to bed and watched TV, but I was still thinking about Boo-Boo. I even fell asleep thinking about Boo-Boo!

The next day I woke up to the sound of Boo-Boo barking. Her bark was loud, squeaky, and overwhelming. WHAT A WAKE UP CALL!

"Come and eat, everyone," my mother shouted. When I got out of bed, I remembered to put on my slippers in case Boo-Boo got close. After breakfast, I went into the bathroom to take a shower, making sure the door was locked so Boo-Boo couldn't get in. After the shower, I put on my clothes, and went to watch TV in the living room.

Oh, oh. Boo-Boo came in the room

"Oh, man, just when I was getting comfortable!" I whined.

I ran out of the room and into the kitchen. Boo-Boo knows not to go in the kitchen. So she stays out, and I stay in, and I stay afraid of dogs.

Hopefully, you noticed that the student did develop the first few scenes of her story with several details. However, the scenes at the end are very short. In fact, the scene that's arguably the most important—the confrontation between the girl and the labradoodle—contains only two sentences. Although her draft does have other issues, focusing the conference on developing all the important parts would be a good decision, especially since her teacher had already identified this as an important need and also focused on this in a recent minilesson.

Scenario Five: The Student Says She's "Done"

One of the most frustrating conference scenarios is when students say they're "done," even though they've made few—if any—revisions to their drafts and have done little or no editing. Often, you'll see they've written "The End" after the last word at the bottom of the page.

Focus these conferences on teaching students about one kind of revision work. Decide what to teach by reading the student's draft and looking for something she's done—or could do—that you've discussed in a recent minilesson or that is connected to one of her needs as a writer.

However, this scenario does present a special challenge. Since students who consider themselves to be finished are often reluctant to do any more work on their drafts, be prepared to encounter some resistance, and be ready to explain the importance of revision. And you'll often need to remind students that you expect them to be the kind of writers who will take risks and try new things—even when they may not feel like it at first.

GRADE 7

A Teacher's Guide to Writing Conferences

Try It Yourself:
Studying Your Conferring

Have several conferences with your students. As you confer, try these strategies to help you discover what they're doing as writers, and assess how well you're supporting your students' talk.

1 Practice beginning your conferences with an open-ended question, followed by some wait time. What do students tell you in response? Which scenarios do you encounter?

2 For students who describe what they're doing very generally, practice asking them to "say more" about what they're doing. Remember to ask them to "say more" several times. How do students' responses evolve? Also, try asking follow-up questions to nudge students to say more, or try naming what they're doing.

3 When you feel you don't want to get behind what students tell you they're doing, practice rebooting the conferences by asking, "What else are you doing?"

4 When students don't say much, try using some of the strategies described in Scenario Three. How do students respond to these strategies?

5 To get ready for Scenarios Four and Five, practice looking at student writing and noticing what kinds of "writing work" students are doing. Pay special attention to things they're doing that are in response to recent minilessons or are connected to what you think are their biggest needs.

6 Record several of your conferences, and as you're watching them afterwards, notice how you invite students to describe what they're doing as writers. What strategies did you use successfully? How could you use the strategies better? What other strategies could you have used?

3

...ASSESS AND decide WHAT TO TEACH...

After you've discovered what a student is doing as a writer, you need to decide what to teach him that will help him be able to do that work better, today and in the future.

- First, as the student talks about what he's doing and you look at his writing, assess how well he's doing his writing work.

- Second, decide what teaching point would help him to do this work better.

PARTS OF A CONFERENCE

CONFERRING MOVES

INTENTIONAL LANGUAGE

DISCOVER what the student is doing as a writer.

Invite the student to tell you what he's doing as a writer.

"How's it going?"

ASSESS how well the student is doing what he's doing, then DECIDE what to teach him.

- Listen to what the student says about what he's doing.
- Look at the student's writing.
- Decide what to teach.

"Let's take a look at your writing . . ."

TEACH the student how to do what he's doing better.

- Give feedback.
- Teach.
- Coach.
- Link to independent work.

- "I want to give you some feedback . . ."
- "I'm going to teach you . . ."
- "Let's try that together . . ."
- "Now I want you to try what we talked about on your own . . ."

The word *assessment* . . . derives from the Latin word *assidere*, meaning to sit alongside.

—PETER JOHNSTON, 1997

Recognizing Patterns Is the Key to Good Decision Making

To understand decision making in writing conferences, it's helpful to step back and think about how we make decisions in other areas of our lives, especially those we make rapidly with some but not a lot of information—just as in a writing conference.

Malcolm Gladwell, in his book *Blink: The Power of Thinking Without Thinking* (2005), writes about "thin-slicing," a concept he describes as a "critical part of rapid cognition." He explains, "'Thin-slicing' refers to the ability of our unconsciousness to find patterns in situations and behavior based on very narrow slices of experience" (23).

This concept of "thin-slicing" helps explain a lot of the decisions we make every day:

1 You glance out the window and notice the sky is overcast and the clouds seem threatening. What will you do?
Decision: Based on the weather pattern, you'll probably bring an umbrella with you.

2 Your toddler is getting cranky after lunch. What will you do?
Decision: You will probably respond to your child's crankiness—a common pattern with small children—by putting her down for a nap.

3 You enter a supermarket and notice that all the shopping carts are in use. What will you do?
Decision: This unlucky pattern means the store is very busy, so you might respond by leaving and coming back later in the day, after running several other errands, in the hope that the store will be less busy then.

In most professions, decision-makers rely on pattern recognition when they make quick decisions.

- NBA point guards recognize patterns—the way the players on the opposing team are arranged on the court—and decide to make certain plays in response, all in a few seconds as they are running down the court.

- A doctor, too, observes patterns—a certain set of symptoms in a patient—so she makes a diagnosis and formulates a treatment plan.

- Even generals recognize patterns—particular ways that enemy troops are positioned on a battlefield—and respond accordingly.

How does this idea of recognizing patterns help you make good decisions about what to teach in a writing conference?

As children grow as writers, they work with partial understandings to "approximate" the different kinds of writing work that experienced writers do. *In Coping with Chaos* (1991), Brian Cambourne and Jan Turbill name teachers' encouragement of approximation—the "franchise to have a go"—as a key characteristic of a "process writing" classroom. Since many young writers make similar approximations, you can think of them as *patterns of approximation*. When you recognize one of these patterns in a writing conference, you can quickly decide what to teach— something that makes the student's partial understanding more complete.

Q&A

IS IT OKAY TO CONFER WITH STRUGGLING WRITERS MORE THAN WITH OTHERS?

ANSWER: Of course. Students who struggle will get more conferences than stronger writers. After all, fairness doesn't mean students get exactly the same amount of time from their writing teachers—fairness means that students get what they need.

Just be careful that you don't *only* confer with struggling writers. I know it's hard to see kids struggle, and there's a lot of pressure to get students to meet standards, but struggling writers need time to work on their writing without you being there. And to move forward, stronger writers need your attention, too.

CARL

ANNA

So how's it going?

Good. My story about my sleepover at Ariane's house is almost finished . . .

So you're writing a sleepover story. What are you doing to write this draft really well?

I'm just trying to stretch it out so it would be a good story.

Say more about that.

I'm just telling about all the details that happened while we were there . . .

All the details that happened when you were there, huh? Let me take a look at your draft . . .

Recognizing Patterns from Student Talk

One way to recognize patterns of approximation is to listen to how students describe what they're doing in the first part of a conference. For example, consider this conference I had with Anna, a second grader:

ANALYSIS

This language hints that she may have written a "bed to bed" story, including everything that happened that night, from beginning to end—a familiar pattern. A quick look at her draft confirms my hunch, and in response I decide to teach her a strategy for focusing a story.

Recognizing Patterns in Student Writing

In many conferences, you'll recognize a pattern of approximation when you look at a student's piece of writing. Take, for example, my conference with Luke, a seventh grader who was writing an argument about why he thought plastic bags should be banned.

In the first part of the conference, Luke told me that although he was citing research in his draft, he wasn't sure how to analyze it. When I asked him, "Why do you think it's important to include your analysis?" he replied, "Because it's on the rubric!" and laughed. Then he continued, "Seriously, I'm not really sure why it's so important. I think the research that I'm writing about is so convincing. Isn't that enough?"

Although I learned from our conversation that Luke was resistant to putting his own analysis of his research into his argument, and that he seemed to be doing this out of compliance ("Because it's on the rubric!"), I didn't yet have enough information to know exactly what I should teach him about analysis.

However, when I skimmed his draft, I quickly saw a pattern of approximation and knew immediately what I needed to teach him:

ANALYSIS

Each time Luke cites research, he responds to it, as writers often do when they write arguments. However, his responses are simplistic, visceral reactions—a common pattern in students learning to write arguments (writing generally rather than specifically is a common pattern in student writing in all genres). He hasn't yet learned how to connect the dots between his research and his claim. For example, at the end of paragraph three, a more experienced writer might have written, "Banning plastic bags would mean there would be less of them in the environment for animals to eat and would remove this terrible threat to animals' health."

Having recognized this pattern, I decide to answer the question Luke was implicitly asking about the importance of analysis in an argument and to teach him how to develop his analysis in a more sophisticated way.

(PART OF) LUKE'S DRAFT

Everywhere I look, I see plastic bags. When I walk through my neighborhood and look up at the beautiful trees, there are plastic bags caught in the branches that the wind has blown there. When I go to Coney Island and swim in the ocean, there are plastic bags floating in the water. These plastic bags are bad for the environment, and should no longer be used in stores. They should be banned, period!

Plastic bags are a serious kind of pollution that litters many of our environments. According to the article, "10 Reasons Why Plastic Bags Should Be Banned" (greentumble.com/10-reasons-why -plastic-bags-should-be-banned/), "Because they are so lightweight, plastic bags can travel long distances by wind and water. They litter our landscapes, get caught in fences and trees, float around in waterways, and can eventually make their way into the world's oceans." This is terrible!

Also, plastic bags are dangerous for animals, who often mistake them for a kind of food. When I read the article, "Why You Should Stop Using Plastic Bags" (thoughtco.com/why-stop-using-plastic -bags-1204167), I learned that thousands of animals die each year from eating plastic bags. "Floating plastic bags regularly fool sea turtles into thinking they are one of their favorite prey, jellyfish." That's awful! And, "This mistaken identity issue is apparently a problem even for camels in the Middle East!" That's really, really terrible! . . .

Writing Patterns and Teaching Points

Experienced writing teachers recognize many patterns of approximation when they confer with student writers, and they know what to teach in response to each of these patterns. How can you build this repertoire of patterns and teaching points? One way is to ask more experienced writing teachers. In this spirit, I'll list some of the most common patterns I see when I confer with students in schools around the world and a possible teaching point for each one. I'll put the patterns into two categories—*writing process* patterns, and *qualities of writing* patterns.

Writing Process Patterns

Many of the lessons you'll teach students are about how to move through the different stages writers go through as they compose:

- rehearsal (or prewriting)
- drafting
- revising
- editing
- publishing.

Rehearsal

Rehearsal includes all the things writers do *before* they actually start work on drafts. This "before work" can make lots of difference in the quality of students' finished work. Before starting drafts, writers

| find topics | gather information about topics |

| figure out what they want to say about topics | plan drafts |

VIDEO

Connor, Grade 7

REHEARSAL PATTERNS	TEACHING POINTS
The student says she has nothing to write about.	Brainstorm topics by making a "Things I Can Write About" list or a "Heart Map" (Heard 2016).
The student has topics to write about but seems to be going through the motions of writing about them without much real interest.	Find topics that spark genuine interest by making lists such as "Unforgettable Memories," "Things I'm an Expert About," or "Issues I Care Strongly About."
The student writes about a series of different topics but doesn't return to any of them again.	Return to favorite topics—what Don Murray (1999) calls "writing territories"—and write about them in different ways. Reread your writing folder to get more ideas about topics you've written about, or make a web of ideas about a topic in your writer's notebook.
The student writes about the same topic but in the same way each time and for the same purpose.	Make a "Heart Map" or a list of the different ways to write about a specific topic. Examples for the topic of baseball might include "The Time I Hit A Home Run," "Best Baseball Players of All Time," and "Why Baseball Coaches Shouldn't Yell."
The student comes up with worthwhile topics but jumps right into writing drafts without developing them.	Develop a topic before drafting by sketching the parts of a story topic across the pages of a book, writing entries in a writer's notebook, or making lists of details about a topic.
The student has gathered some information about her topic, but it's very general ("My trip was really fun," "Elephants look cool," etc.).	Brainstorm specific events (for narrative writing), research specific facts (for informational writing), or research reasons and evidence (for opinion/argument writing).
The student has gathered information about her topic, but isn't sure what she wants to say about it in her draft (Grades 2 and above).	Talk or write in response to the question, "What do I want to say about my topic?" Answering this question will guide you as you think about the point you want to make.
Once the student has gathered information about his topic, he jumps right into his draft without envisioning how he wants it to be structured.	Plan your draft by talking out the piece with a partner, touching each page of a book and saying which part will go on that page (primary), or making a web, flowchart, or outline (upper grades).

TIP

Teaching points need to be appropriate for the grade and experience level of the student you're conferring with—what Lev Vygotsky (1986, 187) calls the student's "zone of proximal development." That is, the specific teaching point should be appropriate for the student's growth as a writer *right now* because with support from you today she'll soon be able to do it herself. The professional resources listed with each set of patterns can help you build a repertoire of teaching points that are appropriate for specific grade levels.

 TEACHING POINT LIBRARY

My books, *Topics* and *Drafts*, which are part of my series, *Strategic Writing Conferences* (C. Anderson 2009), contain conference teaching points that address finding and developing topics, as well as planning drafts. The DVD that comes with the series, *Carl on Camera: Modeling Strategic Writing Conferences*, contains several videos of rehearsal conferences.

Jennifer Serravallo's *The Writing Strategies Book* (2017) contains 300 teaching points for students in grades K–8. The book comprehensively addresses a wide variety of situations you'll encounter with young writers, in every stage of the writing process.

Georgia Heard's *Heart Maps: Helping Students Create and Craft Authentic Writing* (2016) explores how to use "heart maps" to brainstorm and develop ideas in inspiring and deeply felt ways.

Randy Bomer's *Time for Meaning* (1995) has an excellent discussion of what to teach older students who are using writer's notebooks to rehearse ideas.

TEACHING POINT LIBRARY

These books contain teaching points that address drafting and revising: my book *Finished Projects*, which is part of my series, *Strategic Writing Conferences* (C. Anderson 2009); Don Murray's *A Writer Teaches Writing*, 2nd ed. (1985), *The Craft of Revision*, anniversary ed. (2012), and *Write to Learn*, 6th ed. (1999); Sneed B. Collard and Vicki Spandel's *Teaching Nonfiction Revision* (2017); Georgia Heard's *The Revision Toolbox* (2002); Janet Angelillo's *Making Revision Matter* (2005); and Jeff Anderson and Deborah Dean's *Revision Decisions* (2014).

The DVD that comes with *Strategic Writing Conferences*, *Carl on Camera: Modeling Strategic Writing Conferences*, contains several videos of revision conferences.

Drafting and Revising

Although you might think of drafting (composing a piece) and revising (making changes to improve a piece) as separate steps of the writing process, these two steps are closely intertwined. As they're drafting, writers often revise what they've written so far. And as they revise, writers sometimes draft new sections. The boundary between drafting and revising is permeable.

VIDEOS

Skyler, Grade 2

Theo, Grade 8

Maggie, Grade 7

The student is having trouble getting started with a draft.	Use strategies for getting started, such as freewriting a beginning, talking out how the lead could go with a partner, or writing a lead like one in a mentor text.
The student is stuck in the middle of a draft or isn't sure how to get restarted when she returns to a draft.	Get "unstuck" by rereading what you've written so far to spark more ideas or by freewriting whatever comes into your mind until you write a sentence that gets you going again.
The student has an idea of how he would like to craft his writing but isn't sure how to do so.	Look at a mentor text to see how another writer did what you want to do.
The student has finished her draft and written the words "The End" and thinks of herself as "done," even though she has made no revisions to her draft.	Reread your draft and find some places you can improve.
The student wants to make revisions, but has trouble finding places that need revision.	Reread your draft, and put asterisks next to places where you think you can write better, or "box out" the draft (circle each part) and make notes about the changes each part needs.
The student has written a part of her draft but isn't sure if it's good writing.	Get feedback from your writing partner or from a peer conference, or compare your writing to a mentor text.
The student wants to revise, but there is little or no room on the draft to make changes, or she's hesitant to "mess it up."	Use arrows, footnotes, sticky notes, "spiderlegs" (strips of paper added to the draft), or the "cut and paste" functions of a word processing program to make changes to your draft.
The student includes a lot of detail in his writing, but needs to add more that develops his main idea.	Ask yourself, "What else could I add to my piece that would help me get my point across?"
The student reads through his draft from the beginning and makes revisions as they occur to her. However, she may run out of time or run "out of gas" to make needed revisions to the whole draft.	Before making revisions, read through the entire draft and make a revision plan—notes in the margin about possible revisions. Then prioritize the most important ones, and start with those.

. . . Assess and Decide What to Teach . . .

Editing

Although most writers edit their writing as they draft and revise, they usually spend some time concentrating exclusively on editing after they've finished with revision. Writers go on a hunt for anything they've missed—errors in grammar, punctuation, and spelling—and correct them so they won't distract readers.

Editing can be difficult for students. Often they're tired of writing a piece and just want to be finished. Also, editing is tedious work and requires an attention to detail that many students don't yet fully have.

 TEACHING POINT LIBRARY

My book *Finished Projects*, which is part of my series, *Strategic Writing Conferences* (C. Anderson 2009), contains teaching points for editing conferences, and the DVD that comes with the series, *Carl on Camera: Modeling Strategic Writing Conferences*, contains several videos of editing conferences. Jeff Anderson's *Everyday Editing* (2007) contains ideas for teaching points about the editing process.

Lester Laminack and Katie Wood Ray's book *Spelling in Use* (1996) discusses how to address spelling in the writing workshop.

EDITING PATTERNS	TEACHING POINTS
The student's draft contains errors.	Read your draft out loud to yourself, or read it to a classmate in an editing conference.
Two students have exchanged drafts and are reading them silently to themselves.	Read your writing out loud to your peer editor, who will read along and catch errors.
Even after instruction in editing strategies, the student doesn't use the strategies consistently to find mistakes.	Use an "editing checklist" to remind you of the editing strategies you can use.
The student has grammar, punctuation, and/or spelling errors that she continues to make over time, even after instruction on how to do these things correctly.	Create a personalized editing checklist to help you remember to look for your editing "bugaboos" each time you edit.
The student has some spelling errors. ▶ VIDEO Aden, Grade 6	Reread your writing and circle words that don't "look right" (while drafting, revising, or editing). Find support to spell these words correctly: ask someone else, ask "Siri" (on an iPhone), visualize the word in your mind and try spelling it again, or use a dictionary.
The student uses the spell- or grammar-check function on the word processor but doesn't realize that sometimes it identifies words that aren't actually misspelled or fails to identify words that actually are misspelled.	Make one final reread of a draft after using the spell- or grammar-check function.

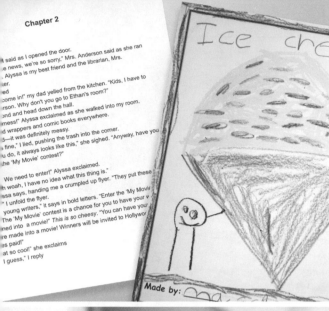

Chapter 2

Publishing

At the very end of the writing process, students publish their writing. Traditionally, this has meant that students make a "final copy" of their drafts to share with others, and perhaps put nice covers on them. Today, with word processers available in many classrooms (mostly in upper grades, once children have acquired keyboarding skills), publishing can be a much more elaborate part of the writing process, with students having the same tools that professional writers and editors use to create beautiful texts.

Publishing also includes the actual sharing of writing with classmates and sometimes with parents who are invited into the classroom for "writing celebrations." Older students may also publish their writing via the internet, on blogs and websites.

TEACHING POINT LIBRARY

Ruth Ayres' book *Celebrating Writers* (2013) and the appendix "Publishing and Celebrating Writing" in Jennifer Serravallo's *The Writing Strategies Book* (2017) have a lot of ideas about how students can publish their writing.

PUBLISHING PATTERNS	TEACHING POINTS
When the student creates a "final copy" for publication, she makes new errors (primarily because the recopying or typing process is boring and tedious).	Read through your final draft to check for unintended recopying errors.
Although the student's final draft is neatly finished, he has made little or no attempt to format the writing so it's visually interesting or pleasing to readers.	Study mentor texts to learn about different publishing options, such as covers, illustrations, and interesting ways to format text.
(Primary) When the student finishes a piece, she puts it in the finished side of her folder without sharing it.	Share your writing with your writing partner or friends in the class.
The student participates in writing celebrations but doesn't seem very interested in getting feedback from classmates.	Identify which students in the class you really want to read your writing, and during the celebration be sure to share with them.
The student has published a piece that would be of interest to people outside the classroom.	Identify people or groups outside the classroom that you can share your writing with, and think about how you might do that (e.g., by mailing letters, emailing pieces to particular people, submitting writing to magazines, or writing a blog).

Qualities of Writing Patterns

You will also teach children about the qualities of writing as they draft, revise, and edit. As students learn how to write pieces that embody these qualities, many of them make similar approximations that we can call *quality of writing patterns*: focus, structure, detail, voice, and conventions.

focus	structure

detail	voice	conventions

Focus

One of the most important qualities of writing is *focus*. Writing is focused when the writer sticks to the same topic across a whole piece. As students get older, focus becomes more complex and challenging, partly because students' writing gets longer, and partly because they're learning more sophisticated ways to "stick to a topic."

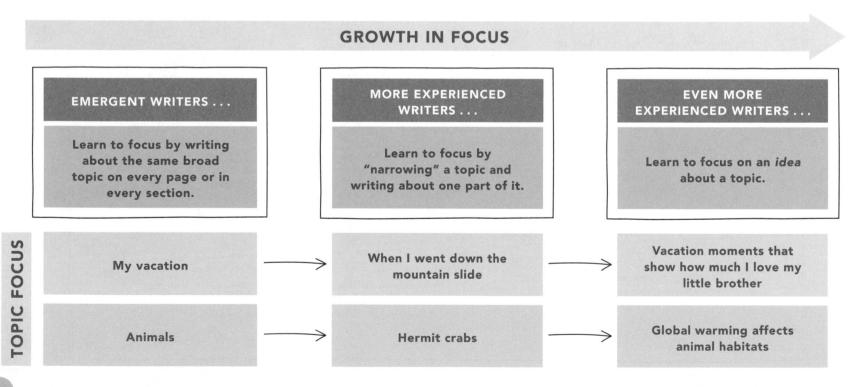

GROWTH IN FOCUS

EMERGENT WRITERS . . .	MORE EXPERIENCED WRITERS . . .	EVEN MORE EXPERIENCED WRITERS . . .
Learn to focus by writing about the same broad topic on every page or in every section.	Learn to focus by "narrowing" a topic and writing about one part of it.	Learn to focus on an *idea* about a topic.

TOPIC FOCUS

My vacation	→	When I went down the mountain slide	→	Vacation moments that show how much I love my little brother
Animals	→	Hermit crabs	→	Global warming affects animal habitats

(Primary) The child communicates primarily through detailed drawings, but they contain so much extraneous detail that it's hard to figure out what the child is writing about.

→ Focus illustrations by including only what is most important in your story (e.g., the main character and what he is doing) or nonfiction book (the subject of the book and what it does).

(Primary) Each page of the student's book is about a different topic. The student understands that writers fill up books with content but does not yet understand that that the content should be about the same topic.

→ Focus by writing or drawing about the same topic on each page of your book.

The student has written a "bed to bed" story including every single detail about an event, or an "all about" nonfiction piece including every single detail she knows about the topic. The student knows how to stick to the topic but not how to narrow it to focus on one part of a story (a "small moment") or nonfiction topic.

→ (Primary) Focus by asking yourself, "What's the part of this event/topic that is most interesting to me?"

(Upper grades) Focus your writing by asking yourself, "What point do I want to make about this topic?" and then include only content that helps you make this point.

The student's draft has a clear focus, but needs specifics to develop the focus.

VIDEO Sofia, Grade 8

→ Develop your focus by including specific events (narrative writing), facts (informational writing), or reasons and examples (opinion/argument writing).

The student's piece is mostly focused, but sometimes it goes off on unnecessary tangents. The student may be writing a long piece with many parts, or a piece about a topic that is new to her, and she doesn't know it well enough yet to maintain focus throughout the piece.

VIDEO Emily, Grade 6

→ Remove pages/sections that don't fit the focus of your writing, or rework sections so they fit your focus.

TEACHING POINT LIBRARY

These books contain lessons on teaching focus, as well as other qualities of writing: my book *Drafts*, which is part of my series, *Strategic Writing Conferences* (C. Anderson 2009); Ralph Fletcher and JoAnn Portalupi's *Craft Lessons: Teaching Writing K–8*, 2nd ed. (2007), *Nonfiction Craft Lessons: Teaching Information Writing K–8* (2001), and *Teaching the Qualities of Writing (Grades 3–6)* (2004); and Jenny Bender's *The Resourceful Writing Teacher* (2007).

The DVD that comes with *Strategic Writing Conferences*, *Carl on Camera: Modeling Strategic Writing Conferences*, contains several videos of conferences which focus on teaching qualities of writing.

Books that have been published on teaching writing to specific grade levels also contain numerous ideas for teaching points about every quality of writing. For primary students: Martha Horn and Mary Ellen Giacobbe's *Talking, Drawing, Writing: Lessons for Our Youngest Writers* (2007); Katie Wood Ray and Matt Glover's *Already Ready: Nurturing Writers in Preschool and Kindergarten* (2008); and Matt Glover's *Engaging Young Writers, Preschool–Grade 1* (2009). For older students: Nancie Atwell's *In the Middle*, 3rd ed. (2014); Randy Bomer's *Time for Meaning: Crafting Literate Lives in Middle and High School* (1995); Laura Robb's *Teaching Middle School Writers: What Every English Teacher Needs to Know* (2010); and Penny Kittle's *Write Beside Them: Risk, Voice, and Clarity in High School Writing* (2008).

Structure

When we read, we expect that the author has structured the text in a way that helps us understand what she's writing about. By *structure*, we mean the parts or sections of a text and the way they're ordered. Leads (introductions) and endings fall into the category of structure, as do transitions, which help readers move from one part of a piece to another.

Narrative and Non-narrative Structures

- In narrative genres (personal narrative, memoir, fiction) we refer to the parts as *scenes*, and they're ordered in time.

- In many non-narrative genres (all-about books, feature articles, op-eds, arguments, essays) we refer to the parts as *chapters* or *subsections* or *subtopics*, and they're ordered by some logic the writer chooses.

STRUCTURE PATTERNS	TEACHING POINTS "As a writer, you can . . ."
(Primary) The student's writing has parts—which may be one sentence each—but she "mushes" all of them into one or two pages of a book, instead of separating the parts on different pages.	→ Separate the parts of your text by putting each one on a different page of your book. You can add more pages if you have a lot of parts.
The way that the student has chosen to order the parts of her piece makes the piece confusing to read.	→ Teach the student how writers in the genre she is writing order the parts of a text.
Although the student is using transitions to guide readers from part to part, he overuses the same one, often "And then . . ."	→ Study mentor texts to notice different kinds of transitions you can use.

TEACHING POINT LIBRARY

Numerous books have been published that focus on the teaching of specific genres; each contains ideas for lessons on structure as well as the other qualities of writing. These include Katherine Bomer's books on teaching memoir and essay, *Writing a Life* (2005) and *The Journey Is Everything* (2016);

Georgia Heard's *Finding the Heart of Nonfiction* (2013) and her books on teaching poetry, *For the Good of the Earth and Sun* (1989) and *Awakening the Heart* (1999); Ralph Fletcher's *Making Nonfiction from Scratch* (2015); Christopher Lehman's *Energize Research Reading and Writing* (2012); Karen Caine's *Writing to Persuade* (2008); Judy Davis and Sharon Hill's *The No-Nonsense Guide to Teaching Writing* (2003); Amy Ludwig VanDerwater's

Poems Are Teachers (2018); and Troy Hicks' *Crafting Digital Writing* (2013). Also, many of the books in curriculum sets, such as Lucy Calkins and colleagues' *Units of Study in Opinion, Information, and Narrative Writing, Grades K–5* (2013) and *Units of Study in Argument, Information, and Narrative Writing, Grades 6–8* (2014) focus on the teaching of specific genres and contain lessons on structure that can be taught in conferences, too.

Each section of a student's piece has the same amount of detail. While the student understands elaboration, she doesn't yet understand that some sections are more important and should be developed more than others.

▶ VIDEO

Ginger, Grade 5

→ (Primary) Identify the parts that feel most important about your topic, and add detail to these parts. (Upper) Identify the parts that are most important to your point, and develop those parts further.

Toward the end of a piece, the student "fizzles"—that is, develops the sections less and less, even though some are important. This usually happens because writers get tired as they get deep into a draft.

→ Revise by identifying important parts, particularly toward the end of your draft, and develop them further.

The student's piece has a series of parts, but the order of the parts doesn't make sense.

→ Study mentor texts to see how writers order parts in the genre in which you're writing.

The student's leads are simplistic ("Hi, my name is David!" or "Do you want to know about rocks?"). He understands writers try to "hook" readers at the beginning, but he doesn't know sophisticated ways to do this, or that leads often let readers know where they're going in the text.

▶ VIDEOS

Jovani, Grade 1

Logan, Grade 6

→ Study mentor texts to find a range of ways to "hook" readers and help them know where they're going in the text.

The student says she doesn't know how to end her piece, or she has written a simplistic ending.

▶ VIDEO

Kiely, Grade 5

→ Study mentor texts to see different ways you can end your piece.

The student includes some structural features of the genre he's writing in his drafts, but not all.

▶ VIDEO

Sam, Grade 4

→ Study mentor texts to see other structural features you could include in your writing (e.g. in narrative, flashbacks; in argument, counterarguments).

TEACHING POINT LIBRARY

Barry Lane's *After the End*, 2nd ed. (2015) and Rozlyn Linder's *The Big Book of Details* (2016) contain a plethora of ideas about teaching detail.

There are many books that discuss the craft of writing that contain ideas for detail teaching points (as well as for other qualities of writing). Two of my favorites are Ralph Fletcher's *What a Writer Needs*, 2nd ed. (2013) and William Zinsser's *On Writing Well*, 25th anniversary ed. (2016). Some of these books discuss how to use mentor texts to teach craft, such as Katie Wood Ray's *Wondrous Words* (1999); Lester Laminack's *Cracking Open the Author's Craft* (2007); Kelly Gallagher's *Write Like This: Teaching Real-World Writing Through Modeling and Mentor Texts* (2011); Allison Marchetti and Rebekah O'Dell's *Writing with Mentors* (2015) and *Beyond Literary Analysis* (2018); and Stacey Shubitz's *Craft Moves* (2016).

Detail

We've all urged children to "add details" to their writing. Teachers know that for students to write well, they need to include the specifics of an event or topic and write about them with precise, concrete details. They also need to learn the different kinds of details writers use in various genres.

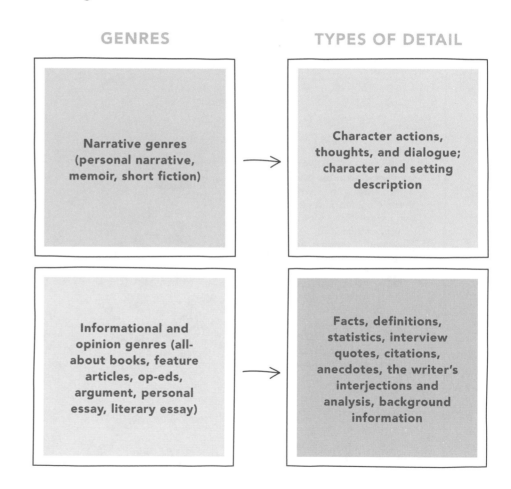

(Primary) The student's illustrations contain some but not all of the kinds of details writers use in the genre.

→ Use a wide variety of details in your illustrations (e.g., in narrative, character actions, expressions, dialogue bubbles).

The student uses only one genre-specific detail in her writing (e.g., in an argument or literary essay, the student uses only citations from texts) or uses just a few.

VIDEOS Urijah, Grade 1 Addison, Grade 3 Ari, Grade 8

→ Add to your repertoire of genre-specific details in your writing. (e.g., add analysis of citations to arguments or literary essays).

The student writes very general details ("I played in the water," "Tigers do a lot of things," or "This shows that Charlotte is a nice character").

VIDEOS  Massimo, Grade K   Jackson, Grade 2   Billy, Grade 3   Henry, Grade 7

→ Break down general details into a series of more specific ones. ("I dove into the water. I held my breath and swam the length of the pool. I was glad when my hand touched the end of the pool." Or "Tigers pounce on their prey, using their strong hind legs to push against the prey and their front legs to knock the prey to the ground.") Or use conjunctions such as *because* to extend thinking ("Charlotte was a clever character because she used her smarts to come up with ways to save Wilbur's life").

The student uses general, not specific, words in her details ("We rode the boat-thingy down the river").

→ Brainstorm or look up more precise words you can use in your details.

The student includes extraneous details that aren't very relevant.

VIDEO  Grace, Grade 7

→ Cut unnecessary detail—or "clutter"—from your writing.

The student's writing reads like a long string of choppy sentences.

→ Use a variety of conjunctions and transitions to connect details to each other.

While the student's writing is finely detailed, she doesn't realize she could more effectively communicate some of that detail in illustrations or graphics.

→ Use illustrations or graphics (diagrams, charts, etc.) to convey information.

. . . Assess and Decide What to Teach . . .

TEACHING POINT LIBRARY

Tom Romano's book *Crafting Authentic Voice* (2004) is full of ideas about teaching voice, particularly in expository writing.

Ralph Fletcher has an excellent discussion of voice in his book *What a Writer Needs*, 2nd ed. (2013).

Katie Wood Ray's *Wondrous Words* (1999) and Dan Feigelson's *Practical Punctuation: Lessons on Rule Making and Rule Breaking in Elementary Writing* (2008) contain ideas on how to teach students to study mentor texts to notice the ways writers use sentence structure and punctuation to create voice.

Voice

When we read a piece of writing, we usually hear the writer's *voice* in it. That is, the sentences have rhythm and cadence, and consequently the piece sounds like human speech written down. And because of the particular "sound" of the writing, we get the sense of the writer's—or the narrator's—personality.

How Writers Create Voice in a Piece of Writing

- Much like composers code a score with notations that let musicians know to play loudly or softly, or quickly or slowly, writers use punctuation marks—exclamation marks, ellipses, dashes, commas, even periods—to give clues to the reader about where to give emphasis in a sentence or where to speed up or slow down.

- By *italicizing* words, making words **bold**, or making words larger than others on the page, writers signal where to give special emphasis to a word or phrase.

- By using certain sentence structures—for example, short sentences, long sentences, or sentences that include a repeated word or phrase—writers also let readers know how to read these sentences.

- Writers sometimes talk directly to readers, addressing them with the pronoun *you* ("When you pick up a rock, you're likely to see several interesting insects crawling underneath"). Or they might ask readers questions—and then answer them ("Have you ever wondered about how big the universe is? . . .").

The student uses punctuation and/or uses upper and lowercase letters conventionally, but not yet in a way to create voice.

→ Read your writing aloud, identify parts you want to sound a certain way, and then use punctuation marks / bold words / italics to signal this to the reader.

The student is so excited about using punctuation marks / bold words / italics to create voice that she overuses the technique throughout her piece.

→ Revise by rereading to check that you've used voice techniques *only* where you really want your writing to sound a particular way.

The student uses simple sentence structures that create a repetitious, flat sound in his writing.

→ Study mentor texts and try out the kinds of sentences you notice that will help your writing "sound" the particular way you want it to sound.

The student's writing has a distant tone.

→ Try addressing the reader directly using the pronoun *you.*

TEACHING POINT LIBRARY

There are numerous professional books that contain ideas for teaching points about conventions, including Jeff Anderson's *Mechanically Inclined* (2005); Mary Ehrenworth and Vicki Vinton's *The Power of Grammar* (2005); Janet Angelillo's *A Fresh Approach to Teaching Punctuation* (2002) and *Grammar Study* (2008); Dan Feigelson's *Practical Punctuation* (2008); Sandra Wilde's *Funner Grammar* (2012); and Amy Benjamin and Barbara Golub's *Infusing Grammar into the Writer's Workshop: A Guide for K–6 Teachers* (2015).

Conventions

Just like experienced writers who are more focused on content and craft as they write, students commonly make distracting errors with the *conventions* of written English. When students edit their writing, they usually find these errors and correct them.

Paradoxically, students also make errors because they're *growing as writers* and trying out more complex sentence structures—structures they encounter when they read, but don't yet know how to punctuate. It helps to reframe your thinking about these errors and recognize them as the result of students approximating these more complex kinds of sentences. These errors are another set of patterns you should be responding to in writing conferences.

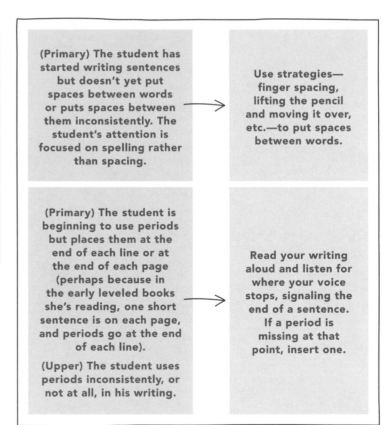

CONVENTION PATTERNS

(Primary) The student has started writing sentences but doesn't yet put spaces between words or puts spaces between them inconsistently. The student's attention is focused on spelling rather than spacing.

(Primary) The student is beginning to use periods but places them at the end of each line or at the end of each page (perhaps because in the early leveled books she's reading, one short sentence is on each page, and periods go at the end of each line).

(Upper) The student uses periods inconsistently, or not at all, in his writing.

TEACHING POINTS "As a writer, you can . . ."

Use strategies—finger spacing, lifting the pencil and moving it over, etc.—to put spaces between words.

Read your writing aloud and listen for where your voice stops, signaling the end of a sentence. If a period is missing at that point, insert one.

The student inconsistently capitalizes the first letter of sentences or doesn't capitalize them at all.  **▶ VIDEO** Liam, Grade 1	Check to make sure that the word following each end mark of punctuation begins with a capital letter.
The student is starting to use conjunctions such as *and* or *but* to write compound sentences. However, he is overusing these conjunctions (especially *and*) and is joining a whole series of clauses together. Sometimes the entire piece is one long "*and* string."	Reread your writing and decide if the conjunctions you've used are necessary. If clauses are closely related ("My father threw the ball, and I caught it"), then keep the conjunction in place. If the clauses have a weak connection ("We drove to the beach and we played in the sand and we swam in the water and we went home"), delete the conjunction and separate the clauses into sentences.
The student is writing sentences with dependent clauses but often puts periods after these clauses, creating sentence fragments.	As you edit, look for sentences with dependent clauses (they start with subordinate conjunctions such as *if*, *after*, or *when*) and check to see if they're punctuated correctly. Commonly writers put commas after dependent clauses, but sometimes they choose to put no punctuation mark after them.
The student is writing sentences with multiple clauses but is having trouble figuring out where these long, complicated sentences end, often joining them with commas (comma splices) or not separating them with punctuation at all.  **▶ VIDEO** Lucine, Grade 4	Read your writing out loud to help you figure out where long, complicated sentences end, and insert an end mark. If a sentence feels like it's getting too long when you read it, figure out somewhere to break it up.
The student misspells frequently used words.	Use a "word wall" or list of high-frequency words as a reference to help you learn how to spell commonly used words.

Try It Yourself: Building Your Knowledge of Writing Patterns and Teaching Points

While the writing patterns I've discussed are the ones I often see and respond to in student writing, this is not a comprehensive list. My hope is that naming these patterns helps you start to see them in your students' writing and imagine how to respond to them. As you grow as a teacher of writing, you'll start to recognize other patterns and figure out how to address them in conferences yourself.

There are several ways you'll do this:

1 Read your students' writing.

- When something surprises you about student work, often it's because you see something that experienced, adult writers wouldn't do. Since approximations are partial understandings, it may be what students are not yet understanding or doing that's surprising you.

- Put what's surprising you into a category. Is it a writing process pattern—something about how students rehearse, draft, revise, edit, or publish? Or is it a quality of writing pattern—an issue of focus, structure, detail, voice, or conventions?

- Describe what students are doing—the pattern —and name what they still need to learn—the teaching point. For example, "Students are telling every single moment of an event from morning to bedtime (pattern) and need to learn that writers choose which events to focus on in a piece (teaching point)." Or "Students are starting to use periods by placing them at the end of lines (pattern) and need to learn how to identify where sentences actually end and put periods there (teaching point)."

2 Look at student writing with colleagues. Ask them to point out patterns they notice, and share what you notice.

3 Writers of professional books on the teaching of writing (such as the authors referenced in this chapter) will often mention patterns they've noticed in student writing.

You might use a chart like this to record the patterns you're finding:

Type of Pattern: Process or Quality of Writing?	Pattern	Possible Teaching Point

...THEN
teach
POWERFULLY

For a conference to help a student grow as a writer, your teaching needs to be top-notch. To accomplish this, you'll make four teaching "moves":

- give feedback
- teach
- coach
- link to independent work.

PARTS OF A CONFERENCE

DISCOVER what the student is doing as a writer.

ASSESS how well the student is doing what he's doing, then DECIDE what to teach him.

TEACH the student how to do what he's doing better.

CONFERRING MOVES

Invite the student to tell you what he's doing as a writer.

- Listen to what the student says about what he's doing.
- Look at the student's writing.
- Decide what to teach.

- Give feedback.
- Teach.
- Coach.
- Link to independent work.

INTENTIONAL LANGUAGE

"How's it going?"

"Let's take a look at your writing . . . "

- "I want to give you some feedback . . . "
- "I'm going to teach you . . . "
- "Let's try that together . . . "
- "Now I want you to try what we talked about on your own . . . "

I believe this naming part of the writing conference is not a throwaway moment, not empty praise, or a pat on the head for being a good girl or boy, but in fact the key to teaching students something they may not have consciously realized they are doing so they can build on it and do it again.

—KATHERINE BOMER, 2010

Move One: Give Feedback

Respond to the Content of Student Writing

Students appreciate getting feedback about the content of their writing. Letting them know that a topic intrigues or moves you is motivating and reassures them that they're writing something worthwhile.

GRADE 1

GRADE 8

Name Students' Strengths

Next, name a strength the student has as a writer to help him become aware of what he's doing successfully. Lucy Calkins, Amanda Hartman, and Zoe White (2005) refer to this kind of feedback as giving students a "lasting compliment" because it helps ensure that what students are doing becomes part of their permanent writing repertoire. Pointing out students' strengths also helps them feel energized as writers, which puts them in a good frame of mind for the teaching that will soon follow.

Point out strengths—or emerging strengths—related to what students are currently learning to do as writers, in response either to recent minilessons or to what you've taught them in previous conferences. This validates the effort students are making to grow as writers, and it helps them see how they're changing.

Be as specific as possible when giving students feedback about their strengths:

INSTEAD OF GIVING GENERAL FEEDBACK . . .

GIVE SPECIFIC FEEDBACK

WORDS FROM
A TEACHING MENTOR

Much more important is noticing—and helping students notice—what they are doing well, particularly the leading edge of what is going well. This leading edge is where the student has reached beyond herself, stretching what she knows just beyond its limit, producing something that is partially correct. This is the launching pad for new learning.

—PETER JOHNSTON, 2004

Giving specific feedback requires you to know enough about what writers do to name what students are doing with precision. Some of the specific language you'll need will come right from minilessons, since many of the things students do are in response to those lessons. But you'll also need to lean on your personal knowledge of writing, as well as what you've learned about what writers do as part of your professional development.

A Teacher's Guide to Writing Conferences

How do you give feedback about students' strengths when they aren't (yet) that strong as writers? The answer is to adopt a "glass is half-full" way of seeing student writers, instead of a "glass is half-empty" perspective. That is, instead of seeing that students are doing things "right" or "wrong" in their writing, understand they're in the process of learning to do things well. Then you'll be able to see—and name—emerging strengths. Seeing that struggling students are taking a few positive steps in their writing—however small—is the key to finding positive things to say and helping them see that they do have emerging strengths, however nascent they may be.

GRADE 1	GRADE 2	GRADE 8

Name One "Next Step"

Finally, set up your teaching point by naming one "next step" students can take as writers and explaining why it makes sense. Be positive and matter-of-fact, especially when you're feeling frustrated because you wish the student already had this next step in her repertoire. The next step optimally builds upon a strength and names what students can do to get even better at something they're already doing:

A Teacher's Guide to Writing Conferences

Putting It All Together

RESPOND TO CONTENT

NAME A STRENGTH

NAME ONE NEXT STEP

For more information about the role of feedback in teaching, see Patty McGee's *Feedback That Moves Writers Forward* (2017).

VIDEOS

Ariana, Grade 1

Ari, Grade 8

Move Two: Teach

The teaching point is the centerpiece of a writing conference. It is where you explain what it is that you want the student to learn about writing, and how to do it.

Cue the Student

Begin teaching points by cueing the student that you're starting to teach: *Today I'm going to teach you* . . . Then, name the specific strategy, craft, or convention you're going to teach: . . . *how to begin a feature article with an anecdote*. Other ways that you can signal the beginning of the teaching point include:

- *Something experienced writers do that I want to discuss with you is* . . .

- *Today I'd like to show you that* . . .

- *Here's something that I'd like you to learn about writing, which is called* . . .

Each of these phrases signals that students should get ready to learn something new about writing and should focus on the one—and only one—thing you're going to teach in the conference.

Explain What You're Teaching

Your explanation should include:

A DEFINITION OF WHAT YOU'RE TEACHING.	AN EXPLANATION OF WHY IT'S IMPORTANT TO LEARN.	YOU MIGHT INCLUDE A METAPHOR.
Definitions are always helpful, especially when you're introducing an aspect of writing you haven't yet discussed in a minilesson or previous conference with the student.	Students typically embrace teaching if they understand the *why* behind it, and will use what you teach them more purposefully.	When you're teaching something that you think will be a challenge, metaphors can help students understand the teaching point. By connecting your teaching to something familiar, you'll help students grasp and understand why writers do the things they do.
EXAMPLE: *A topic sentence is a sentence that previews what you're going to write about in a paragraph or section.*	**EXAMPLE:** *Topic sentences signal the reader that you're about to discuss another point about your topic.*	**EXAMPLE:** *Just like teachers say, "Class, it's now time for math!"—which lets you know what you'll be doing during the next class period—a topic sentence lets readers know what the writer will be discussing in the next part of a piece.*

To find and teach with excellent mentor texts, consider these tips:

- Gather texts (picture books, collections, pieces from magazines, newspapers, websites, etc.) in the genres your students will be writing across the year.

- Look for well-written texts that you and your students will enjoy reading.

- Study each text closely and identify the many things you can teach with it—the way the author organized it, wrote the lead and ending, transitioned from part to part, elaborated with different kinds of details, used voice techniques, and so on.

- Carry a few good mentor texts with you as you confer.

Then show an example of what you're teaching, using just **one** of these methods:

DEMONSTRATE A WRITING STRATEGY.	SHOW WRITER'S NOTEBOOKS OR DRAFTS.
When you're teaching a strategy to help a student move through a stage of the writing process, explain the strategy and then do it yourself while the student watches.	To give students an image of what writers do at a stage of the writing process, show your own (or another student's) writer's notebook or a draft with revisions or edits visible.

EXAMPLES:
(Drafting) *I'm going to show you how I sound out a word, listen for the sounds, and figure out what letter goes with that sound . . .* (Editing) *I'm going to show you how I edit my writing by reading it aloud and looking and listening for mistakes as I do this . . .*

EXAMPLES:
Let's take a look at some pages of my writer's notebook where I gathered facts to use in my feature article . . . or Here's a draft of my story about going to the beach. I want you to see how I used sticky notes to add details to several pages . . .

  VIDEO Aden, Grade 6

  VIDEO Maggie, Grade 7

SHARE A MENTOR TEXT.

When you're teaching a craft technique, show it to students in a text by a well-known author or in one written by yourself or a student.

EXAMPLES:
I'm going to point out the way this author wove action, thoughts and feelings, and dialogue together when she wrote her scenes, so that you can get an image of how you can do this in your own writing . . .

 VIDEO Matthew, Grade 4

ASK STUDENTS TO STUDY A MENTOR TEXT.

Ask students to study a mentor text. Asking students to do this helps them develop and strengthen the habit of mind Frank Smith (1987) and Katie Wood Ray (1999) call "reading like a writer," a kind of "close reading" experienced writers do to build their craft knowledge. Students will usually notice some of what the writer has done, and then you'll fill in what they aren't able to see.

EXAMPLES:
Take a look at the ending of this op-ed, which I've circled. What do you notice about the way the author wrote it?

 VIDEO Jovani, Grade 1

Q&A

SHOULD I WRITE MY OWN MENTOR TEXTS? USE STUDENT EXAMPLES?

ANSWER: Writing your own mentor texts has several benefits. First, there are some kinds of writing that are just hard to find for kids, such as literary essays, so writing your own is the best way to have some on hand. Second, writing mentor texts reminds you of the challenges of writing in a particular genre—and of writing in general—and this will help you confer with more understanding and empathy. Third, when you use your own writing as a mentor text, you'll find that students love what you write and see you not just as a writing teacher but as a writing teacher who is a "real" writer.

You can also use a piece of student writing as a mentor text. Students love to see their classmates' writing, which is usually closer to their level, so they may feel more confident trying out what they see. And if the student mentor is socially powerful, some students will want to do similar work so they can be more like that student.

Explain How to Do What You're Teaching

To conclude a teaching point, you'll explain how writers do what you're teaching—that is, you'll describe a strategy the student can use:

> **EXAMPLE:**
>
> Writers figure out the point of their piece *by asking themselves, "What do I want to say about this topic?"*

> **EXAMPLE:**
>
> Writers plan out a book *by touching each page and saying what part of their story/topic they're going to write on that page.*

> **EXAMPLE:**
>
> Writers check to see that their writing is focused *by reading each part of a piece and asking themselves, "Does this part have to do with my topic/big idea?"*

> **EXAMPLE:**
>
> Writers write precise character actions *by visualizing a character in their heads and "seeing" what the character is doing with her hands, her legs, her face, and with the other parts of her body.*

> **EXAMPLE:**
>
> Writers decide to use italics to give their writing voice *by reading their drafts aloud and listening for which words they read with more excitement and emphasis.*

> **EXAMPLE:**
>
> Writers figure out where sentences end—and where they need end marks—*by reading their writing out loud and listening to where they make full stops.*

The idea is to add to the young writer's repertoire of strategies—not merely to improve a particular piece of writing, but to improve *all* the writing that student will do.

—RALPH FLETCHER AND JOANN PORTALUPI, 2001b

TIP

Many of the strategies you'll teach will be ones that you use when you write. You may need to ask yourself, "How exactly do I do this?" to help you think about this. Also, many of the professional books listed in Chapter 3 include strategies you can teach.

I've noticed that many teachers don't include strategies in their teaching points. I think this is because the things we teach students about writing are things that we, as experienced adult writers, know how to do automatically— that is, we aren't conscious anymore of how we do these things when we do them. Thus, it doesn't occur to us that students, who will be trying something for the first time, need to be taught how to deliberately and consciously think about how to do something, and that it will take them some time to internalize a strategy before it becomes automatic.

Move Three: Coach

After the teaching point, you'll coach the student as she tries the strategy. Much like my dad held onto the back of my bicycle and ran beside me before I was able to ride on my own, the brief "try it" part of the conference is an assisted performance.

The point of the "try it" isn't for the student to complete the work or to "master" what you've taught. The point is for the student to get enough of a feel for the strategy to be able to continue doing it on her own after the conference.

Often, students can try out the strategy by talking through what they will do. An oral "try it" gives you a quick sense of students' understanding and the coaching they may need from you. Of course, sometimes it makes sense for students to do some writing. For example, if you're a primary teacher, when you teach your students to put spaces between their words, you'll have them try this with their pencils, since the strategy is a physical one.

Begin this part of the conference by saying, *Let's try this together*, then asking open-ended questions, such as *Where could you try this in your piece?* and then *How could you try what I just taught you in this part?* Then stop talking and give students a chance to think and respond. Hopefully, their responses will show enough understanding that you can end the conference and give them the opportunity to apply what you taught on their own.

Sometimes, however, students respond tentatively, or even with a shrug. In these conferences, you'll coach students by helping them use the strategy you just taught.

VIDEOS

Ariana, Grade 1

Sam, Grade 4

Shreya, Grade 5

When students have some difficulty with the "try it," it's all too easy to ask leading questions that guide them to write what you think they should write. Avoid this because leading questions, however well intentioned, take decisions away from students, decisions they ultimately need to learn to make on their own, however challenging these decisions may be at this point in their development. If you make decisions for students, then they won't know how to make them in their next piece of writing, and you're back to square one when you confer with them again.

. . . Then Teach Powerfully

Move Four:
Link to Independent Work

Finally, let students know that you expect them to do what you taught right away—that is, link the conference to students' independent work. Students don't learn how to do what you teach them until they try it in their writing.

You might say, *What are you going to do now?* or *Tell me what your plans are for your writing now.*

Or you might rename the teaching point and tell students exactly what you want them to do once the conference is over. For example, *I want you to try writing a counterargument now.*

End the conference with a reminder and a promise: *This is something you'll be able to use today and in your future writing. I'll be back after my next conference to see how this goes. Go for it!"*

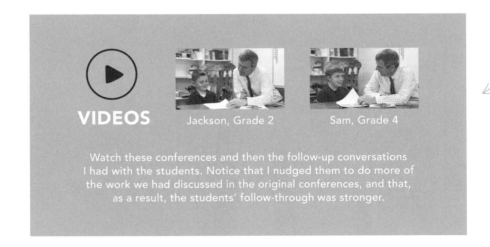

VIDEOS   Jackson, Grade 2   Sam, Grade 4

Watch these conferences and then the follow-up conversations I had with the students. Notice that I nudged them to do more of the work we had discussed in the original conferences, and that, as a result, the students' follow-through was stronger.

TIP

Try these strategies to encourage students to follow through with your teaching:

- Some students may need you to stay until they get started. Take advantage of this time to make conference notes, then leave.

- Some students may need you to stay a few extra minutes and coach them as they try what you taught them to do as they write.

- If a student is easily distracted, you might write a note to remind her of a teaching point and the work she's going to do. Don't waste precious time doing this, however, if you see that students don't need this support.

- Check back *after your next conference* to see what a student has done in response to your teaching. If too much time passes, students may not remember as clearly what they did, and you can't reteach as easily if they didn't understand.

- If you find out a student *hasn't* tried what you taught, offer a quick, direct reminder that you expect her to try.

- To encourage future follow-through, you might write a reminder on a student conference record sheet.

Name _____ Ben _____

CONFERENCE NOTES

Date	Remember to . . .
9/8	Write about your favorite topics — you said, "My family, sports, Cape Cod."
9/16	Focus by writing about the part of a topic that interests you.
9/22	Revise by rereading your writing and asking yourself, "What else can I say here?"
9/25	Editing: listen for when your voice stops when you read aloud. Put periods there!

Studying the Four Teaching Moves in a Transcript of a Conference

Let's take a look at a conference I had with a third-grade student. In the first part of the conference, I learned that he was trying to develop the scenes of his story about hitting a home run by adding "character actions"—that is, by describing what he and the pitcher were doing with their bodies in the story. When I skimmed his draft, I saw that the actions he had included were general ("I was up at bat and hit a home run"), and it was hard for me to get a detailed picture in my mind of what happened. Thus, I decided to teach him how to write precise actions.

In the transcript, I have annotated the four teaching moves: give feedback, teach, coach, and link to independent work.

(1) Give feedback. (a) First, I let him know that I think his story is an exciting one. **(b)** Then I give him feedback about one of his writing strengths. **(c)** And then I give him feedback about a "next step" he can take.

(2) Teach. (a) First, I cue the student that I'm teaching and name what I'm going to teach. **(b)** I define what I mean by exact character actions.

(c) Then I use a metaphor to help the student understand their importance.

(d) I show the student some examples of different kinds of character actions in a mentor text.

(1) I have some feedback for you. **(a)** First of all, what an exciting moment this was for you, when you hit that home run! I think that readers are going to enjoy learning about this moment in your life. **(b)** I see you are trying to include some character actions in your story, especially what you and the pitcher did when you were at bat and hit the home run. **(c)** It would be a good thing for you to learn how to write actions in a way that readers can "see" them better in their minds, since the ones you've written are general—that is, it's hard for me to really get a picture in my mind of what you and the pitcher were doing.

(2) (a) So today I want to teach you how to write exact actions when you write stories. **(b)** Exact actions are what characters do with parts of their bodies. They can be what a character is doing with his feet, like skipping or running. Or they can be what a character is doing with his tongue, such as sticking it out so a doctor can look at his throat.

(c) Exact actions help readers "see" what's happening in a story when they read it, as if they're watching a movie or a TV show. If there weren't exact actions in a story, it would be like watching a movie and seeing nothing on the screen. That's how important they are to a story.

(d) Let's look at a page from Julie Brinckloe's *Fireflies!* to see how an experienced writer puts exact actions in a story. (I open up the picture book and start to read.)

We ran like crazy, barefoot in the grass.
"Catch them, catch them!" we cried, grasping at the lights . . .
. . . I thrust my hand into the jar and spread it open. The jar glowed like moonlight and I held it in my hands.

As I read this part, I bet you could "see" the kids running outside and the main character putting a firefly into a jar, couldn't you? The reason you could "see" what they were doing is because Julie Brinckloe described what the kids did with their feet (they "ran like crazy") and hands (the main character thrust his hand into the jar).

Another kind of action is the kind people do with parts of their faces—their mouths, their eyes, their tongues. Julie Brinckloe wrote these kinds of actions, too, at the end of the story where the main character lets all the fireflies go. (I read from another page in the text.)

> I held the jar . . . in my hands.
> The moonlight and the fireflies swam in my
>   tears, but I could feel myself smiling.

In this part, Julie Brinckloe told us what the main character was doing with his eyes—he was crying—and what he was doing with his mouth—he was smiling.

(e) To write exact character actions, writers try to "see" their story in their mind, like a movie. As they watch this "movie," they zoom in close to each character and think about what he is doing with his legs, his hands, and his face. Then they write these details in their story.

(e) I describe a strategy for how writers come up with exact character actions.

(4) Link to independent work. (a) I tell the student that I want him to try what I taught in his writing. (b) I let him know that this is something he can add to his writing repertoire. (c) And then I let him know I'll be back soon to see how he does with the work.

(3) Coach.
(a) When the student has some difficulty coming up with exact actions, I coach him by guiding him through the strategy I discussed in the teaching point (2.e).

(3) Let's try this together.

Me: In the part of the story that you're writing, in which you were up at bat, what were you doing exactly?
Student: I was standing at home plate.
Me: And?
Student: (doesn't answer)
(a) Me: What exactly were you doing with your legs as you stood there?
Student: My legs were spread wide.
Me: Good. What were you doing with your hands?
Student: I was gripping the bat really tight. I was holding it in launch position.
Me: And what were you doing with your face?
Student: I was smiling! I love being at bat.
Me: Fantastic! I think you're getting the hang of thinking of exact character actions. I'm getting a much better picture of what you did in this part of the story.

(4) Now I'd like you to continue writing your story. (a) As you work, try to write these kinds of exact character actions to describe what you did, as well as what the pitcher did. (b) This is a great thing to learn how to do as a writer—you'll want to do this in any story you write, from now on. (c) I'll be back in a few minutes to see how you do with this work. Off you go!

Q&A

HOW SHOULD I TAKE NOTES ON CONFERENCES?

ANSWER: The are lots of tools for note-taking, and you will need to find one that works for you. What's most important is that you think about the kinds of notes you need to record. Here are two examples of conferring notes:

Notice that the teacher wrote down the date, the topic the student was writing about, an observation, and the teaching point for this conference.

CLASS CONFERENCE NOTES   Dates: 9/8 to ____

Syeda - 9/8 not sure what to write about (T) make a list of favorite topics	Eduard - 9/12 dog story "I'm done!" (T) revise by adding onto draft	Stacey - 9/9 "all about" Cape Cod story (T) focus on a small moment	Raymond -	Haskell - 9/10 wants to add details to fishing story - his details are general (T) write exact actions	Danya - 9/11 beach story - all parts even length (T) develop imp parts
Anita - 9/11 skunk story unnecessary 1st scene (T) start close to problem	Nate - 9/9 camp story 1-2 details per part (T) elab with bit-by-bit action	Tiffany A. -	Jemel - 9/10 "all-about" trip to SC (T) focus on small moment	Demeka - 9/12 cat story wants to revise lead (T) dialogue lead	Ethan -
Leo - 9/9 beach story lots of dialogue (T) mix action & feeling into dialogue	Kamara -	Erik - 9/11 baseball story abrupt ending (T) end story with reflection	Tiffany N. 9/12 dad story "I'm done!" (T) revise by adding on	Wyatt - 9/8 jumped right into home run story (T) plan by making flow chart	Josh - 9/11 revising story about play - no room for add-ons (T) use tools-carets arrows- to add on
Atticus - 9/12 skiing story fizzles by end (T) stretch all important parts	Evie - 9/8 not sure what to write about (T) make a heart map	Kaelyn - 9/10 lots of character details (T) choose telling character details	Henry - 9/9 playground story - lots of actions (T) add thoughts/feelings	Sylvie - 9/8 "all about" softball game (T) focus on small moment	Bonnie -

It's easy to tell which students to confer with next, because their boxes are still blank.

This form is used to record notes about several conferences with one student.

Student __Maggie__   Dates __9/12 – 10/12__

Conference Notes	Next Steps
9/12 isn't sure what to write about (T) make a list of favorite topics / writing territories	- Write about favorite topics (she said, "My cat, family & friends")
9/25 draft of story, "When I Got My Cat" - "all about" draft - a few periods in piece (T) focus on a small moment	- focus - end sentences with periods
10/2 peer editing with Sage - they exchanged papers and were reading silently (T) writer reads aloud to editor in editing conference	- peer editing strategies
10/12 researching cats for feature article - collecting facts about many aspects of cats (T) focus on one part of topic	- focus

Notice that the teacher wrote down the date, the topic the child was writing about, observations, and the teaching point for this conference.

Based on what the teacher learned in each conference, she wrote down "next steps" to guide future conferences with the student.

To keep track of which students have had conferences, the teacher using this form also used the Student Conference Record in Chapter 2, p. 27.

Try It Yourself: Improving Your Conference Teaching

With these simple exercises, you can practice the four teaching moves before actually conferring with students. Ultimately, you'll gain skill by practicing the moves with students, over and over, until they become part of your conferring repertoire.

1 Read a piece of student writing and identify an issue you might address in a writing conference. Write out what you would say to teach this student, including all four moves (you'll have to imagine what the student might say during the third move!). When you finish, reread what you've written and annotate each of the four moves. Reread the sections on the moves in this chapter, and then make revisions to improve what you wrote. By doing this exercise once—or several times—you will get the feel for the teaching and can then step into actual conferences with more confidence.

2 Role-play a teaching point with a colleague, preferably one who has also read this chapter. Give each other feedback about the moves after the role-play is over.

3 Use your smartphone or iPad to video a few of your conferences with students. Later on, watch them and assess which of the four moves you made most successfully and which ones need work.

4 Ask a fellow teacher, coach, or principal who has read this chapter to visit your classroom and watch you confer. Afterwards, ask the observer to name the moves you made and make suggestions for how you could improve your conference teaching.

Works Cited

Allyn, Pam. 2012a. *Core Ready Lesson Sets for Grades K–2*. New York: Pearson.

———. 2012b. *Core Ready Lesson Sets for Grades 3–5*. New York: Pearson.

Anderson, Carl. 2009. *Strategic Writing Conferences*. Portsmouth, NH: Heinemann *first*Hand.

Anderson, Jeff. 2005. *Mechanically Inclined*. Portland, ME: Stenhouse.

———. 2007. *Everyday Editing*. Portland, ME: Stenhouse.

Anderson, Jeff, and Deborah Dean. 2014. *Revision Decisions*. Portland, ME: Stenhouse.

Angelillo, Janet. 2002. *A Fresh Approach to Teaching Punctuation*. New York: Scholastic.

———. 2005. *Making Revision Matter*. New York: Scholastic.

———. 2008. *Grammar Study*. New York: Scholastic.

Atwell, Nancie. 2014. *In the Middle*. 3rd ed. Portsmouth, NH: Heinemann.

Ayres, Ruth. 2013. *Celebrating Writers*. Portland, ME: Stenhouse.

Ball, Deborah. 2015. Interview by Emily Handford. "Rethinking Teacher Preparation." *American Radioworks*, August 27. www.americanradioworks.org/segments/rethinking-teacher-preparation/.

Bender, Jenny. 2007. *The Resourceful Writing Teacher*. Portsmouth, NH: Heinemann.

Benjamin, Amy, and Barbara Golub. 2015. *Infusing Grammar into the Writer's Workshop: A Guide for K–6 Teachers*. New York: Routledge.

Bomer, Katherine. 2005. *Writing a Life*. Portsmouth, NH: Heinemann.

———. 2010. *Hidden Gems*. Portsmouth, NH: Heinemann.

———. 2016. *The Journey Is Everything*. Portsmouth, NH: Heinemann.

Bomer, Randy. 1995. *Time for Meaning: Crafting Literate Lives in Middle and High School*. Portstmouth, NH: Heinemann.

Brinckloe, Julie. 1985. *Fireflies*. New York: Aladdin Books.

Caine, Karen. 2008. *Writing to Persuade*. Portsmouth, NH: Heinemann.

Calkins, Lucy. 1986. *The Art of Teaching Writing*. 1st ed. Portsmouth, NH: Heinemann.

———. 1994. *The Art of Teaching Writing*. New ed. Portsmouth, NH: Heinemann.

———. 2013. *A Guide to the Common Core Writing Workshop*. Portsmouth, NH: Heinemann *first*Hand.

Calkins, Lucy, Amanda Hartman, and Zoe White. 2005. *One to One*. Portsmouth, NH: Heinemann.

Calkins, Lucy, and colleagues. 2013. *Units of Study in Opinion, Information, and Narrative Writing, Elementary Series Bundle, Grades K–5*. Portsmouth, NH: Heinemann.

———. 2014. *Units of Study in Argument, Information, and Narrative Writing, Middle School Series Bundle, Grades 6–8*. Portsmouth, NH: Heinemann.

Cambourne, Brian, and Jan Turbill. 1991. *Coping with Chaos*. Portsmouth, NH: Heinemann.

Collard, Sneed B., and Vicki Spandel. 2017. *Teaching Nonfiction Revision*. Portsmouth, NH: Heinemann.

Cruz, M. Colleen. 2004. *Independent Writing*. Portsmouth, NH: Heinemann.

Davis, Judy, and Sharon Hill. 2003. *The No-Nonsense Guide to Teaching Writing*. Portsmouth, NH: Heinemann.

Ehrenworth, Mary, and Vicki Vinton. 2005. *The Power of Grammar*. Portsmouth, NH: Heinemann.

Feigelson, Dan. 2008. *Practical Punctuation: Lessons on Rule Making and Rule Breaking in Elementary Writing*. Portsmouth, NH: Heinemann.

———. 2014. *Reading Projects Reimagined*. Portsmouth, NH: Heinemann.

Fletcher, Ralph. 2013. *What a Writer Needs*. 2nd ed. Portsmouth, NH: Heinemann.

———. 2015. *Making Nonfiction from Scratch*. Portland, ME: Stenhouse.

Fletcher, Ralph, and JoAnn Portalupi. 2001a. *Nonfiction Craft Lessons: Teaching Information Writing K–8*. Portland, ME: Stenhouse.

———. 2001b. *Writing Workshop: The Essential Guide*. Portsmouth, NH: Heinemann.

———. 2004. *Teaching the Qualities of Writing*. Portsmouth, NH: Heinemann *first*Hand.

———. 2007. *Craft Lessons: Teaching Writing K–8*. 2nd ed. Portland, ME: Stenhouse.

Fu, Danling. 2009. *Writing Between Languages*. Portsmouth, NH: Heinemann.

Gallagher, Kelly. 2011. *Write Like This: Teaching Real-World Writing Through Modeling and Mentor Texts*. Portland, ME: Stenhouse.

Gladwell, Malcolm. 2005. *Blink: The Power of Thinking Without Thinking*. New York: Little, Brown.

Glover, Matt. 2009. *Engaging Young Writers, Preschool–Grade 1*. Portsmouth, NH: Heinemann.

Glover, Matt, and Mary Alice Berry. 2012. *Projecting Possibilities for Writers*. Portsmouth, NH: Heinemann.

Graves, Donald. 1981. *Final Report: A Case Study Observing the Development of Primary Children's Composing, Spelling and Motor Behaviors During the Writing Process*. Durham, NH: Writing Process Laboratory, University of New Hampshire.

———. 1983. *Writing: Teachers and Children at Work*. Portsmouth, NH: Heinemann.

Hattie, John. 2009. *Visible Learning*. New York: Routledge.

Heard, Georgia. 1989. *For the Good of the Earth and Sun*. Portsmouth, NH: Heinemann.

———. 1999. *Awakening the Heart*. Portsmouth, NH: Heinemann.

———. 2002. *The Revision Toolbox*. Portsmouth, NH: Heinemann.

———. 2013. *Finding the Heart of Nonfiction*. Portsmouth, NH: Heinemann.

———. 2016. *Heart Maps: Helping Students Create and Craft Authentic Writing*. Portsmouth, NH: Heinemann.

Hicks, Troy. 2013. *Crafting Digital Writing*. Portsmouth, NH: Heinemann.

Horn, Martha, and Mary Ellen Giacobbe. 2007. *Talking, Drawing, Writing: Lessons for Our Youngest Writers*. Portland, ME: Stenhouse.

Johnston, Peter H. 1997. *Knowing Literacy*. Portland, ME: Stenhouse.

———. 2004. *Choice Words*. Portland, ME: Stenhouse.

Kaufman, Douglas. 2000. *Conferences and Conversations*. Portsmouth, NH: Heinemann.

Keene, Elin. 2012. *Talk About Understanding*. Portsmouth, NH: Heinemann.

Kittle, Penny. 2008. *Write Beside Them: Risk, Voice, and Clarity in High School Writing*. Portsmouth, NH: Heinemann.

Laman, Tasha Tropp. 2013. *From Ideas to Words*. Portsmouth, NH: Heinemann.

Laminack, Lester. 2007. *Cracking Open the Author's Craft*. New York: Scholastic.

Laminack, Lester, and Katie Wood Ray. 1996. *Spelling in Use*. Urbana, IL: NCTE.

Lane, Barry. 2015. *After the End*. 2nd ed. Portsmouth, NH: Heinemann.

Lehman, Christopher. 2012. *Energize Research Reading and Writing*.
　　Portsmouth, NH: Heinemann.

Linder, Rozlyn. 2016. *The Big Book of Details*. Portsmouth, NH: Heinemann.

Marchetti, Allison, and Rebekah O'Dell. 2015. *Writing with Mentors*.
　　Portsmouth, NH: Heinemann.

———. 2018. *Beyond Literary Analysis*. Portsmouth, NH: Heinemann.

McGee, Patty. 2017. *Feedback That Moves Writers Forward*. Thousand Oaks,
　　CA: Corwin.

Mermelstein, Leah. 2013. *Self-Directed Writers*. Portsmouth, NH: Heinemann.

Murray, Donald. 1985. *A Writer Teaches Writing*. 2nd ed. New York: Houghton
　　Mifflin Harcourt.

———. 1999. *Write to Learn*. 6th ed. New York: Harcourt Brace.

———. 2012. *The Craft of Revision*. Anniversary ed. Belmont, CA: Wadsworth.

Ray, Katie Wood. 1999. *Wondrous Words*. Urbana, IL: NCTE.

Ray, Katie Wood, and Matt Glover. 2008. *Already Ready: Nurturing Writers in
　　Preschool and Kindergarten*. Portsmouth, NH: Heinemann.

Robb, Laura. 2010. *Teaching Middle School Writers: What Every English
　　Teacher Needs to Know*. Portsmouth, NH: Heinemann.

———. 2012. *Practical Units for Teaching Middle School Writers*. Portsmouth,
　　NH: Heinemann.

Romano, Tom. 2004. *Crafting Authentic Voice*. Portsmouth, NH: Heinemann.

Serravallo, Jennifer. 2017. *The Writing Strategies Book*. Portsmouth, NH:
　　Heinemann.

Smith, Frank. 1987. *Joining the Literacy Club*. Portsmouth, NH: Heinemann.

Shubitz, Stacey. 2016. *Craft Moves*. Portland, ME: Stenhouse.

VanDerwater, Amy Ludwig. 2018. *Poems Are Teachers*. Portsmouth, NH:
　　Heinemann.

Vygotsky, Lev. 1986. *Thought and Language*. Edited by Alex Kozulin.
　　Cambridge, MA: MIT Press.

Wagner, Tony. 2008. *The Global Achievement Gap*. New York: Basic Books.

Wilde, Sandra. 2012. *Funner Grammar*. Portsmouth, NH: Heinemann.

Zinsser, William. 2016. *On Writing Well*. 25th anniversary ed. New York:
　　Harper Collins.

Also Available from

THE CLASSROOM ESSENTIALS SERIES

With fresh and engaging content, books in the Classroom Essentials series bring the transformative power of foundational ideas and student-centered practices to today's busy teachers.

A Teacher's Guide to Getting Started with Beginning Writers

Katie Wood Ray with Lisa Cleaveland

In Lisa Cleaveland's classroom, writing workshop is a time every day when her students make books. Katie Wood Ray guides you through the first days in Lisa's classroom, offering ideas, information, strategies, and tips that show, step by step, how you can launch writing workshop with beginning writers.

If you're a new teacher or new to writing workshop, *A Teacher's Guide to Getting Started with Beginning Writers* will show you in clear and simple terms what to do to establish a routine for writing in your classroom, offering you vision, insight, and practical support. If you're an experienced workshop teacher, Katie and Lisa will help you imagine new possibilities.

Grades K–2 / 978-0-325-09914-9 / 2018

HOW CAN I ESTABLISH A ROUTINE FOR WRITING IN MY CLASSROOM?

WHY IS MAKING BOOKS DEVELOPMENTALLY APPROPRIATE?

HOW CAN I HELP MY YOUNGEST STUDENTS BECOME WRITERS?

Visit Heinemann.com/ClassroomEssentials for up-to-date information about other available titles in the Classroom Essentials series.

Includes more than 25 classroom videos!

THE CLASSROOM ESSENTIALS SERIES
With fresh and engaging content, books in the Classroom Essentials series bring the transformative power of foundational ideas and student-centered practices to today's busy teachers.

How can I get started with conferring or improve my conferences?

How can I fit conferences into my busy writing workshop schedule?

How can conferences help me meet the diverse needs of student writers?

Carl Anderson is an internationally recognized expert in writing instruction for grades K–8. He works as a consultant in schools and districts around the world, and is a longtime staff developer for the Teachers College Reading and Writing Project. Carl is the author of numerous books on teaching writing, including the best-selling *How's It Going? A Practical Guide to Conferring with Student Writers.*

Helping students become better writers is what writing conferences are all about. In *A Teacher's Guide to Writing Conferences*, Carl Anderson explains the underlying principles and reasons for conferring with students, and how to make writing conferences a part of your daily routine. With clear and accessible language, Carl guides you through the three parts of a writing conference and shows you the teaching moves and intentional language to use in each one. Classroom video plus teaching tips bring the content to life and provide everything you need to become a better writing teacher.

Heinemann
DEDICATED TO TEACHERS™

www.heinemann.com

ISBN 978-0-325-09918-7
90000 >
9 780325 099187

T4-AYS-187